What priority do you give your relationship with money—earning, spending, and saving? Next to food and eating, money is your most sought after energy source; with the former being difficult to attain without the latter. Nance and Charlesworth's *Mind Over Money* uniquely reveals how critical and mutable this relationship is over the course of your lifetime. WHY and HOW you spend your money (and others') must be balanced in terms of mental, emotional, and fiscal realities. You'll find *Mind Over Money's* innovative "blueprints" to be well worth the time and money you invest today.

— Kathy S. Scverow, M.S., M.Ed.
President, PowerInc Corp.
Author, *PsychoNutrition: D.I.E.T.*
for the 21st Century

Reading Wayne Nance's *Mind Over Money* is an insurance policy against financial failure. It will help anyone avoid the all too common pitfalls, mistakes and errors people make. Applying just one of the ideas in the book would yield a tremendous profit for the reader.

— Wilson J. Humber, PhD.
Author, *Dollars & Sense*

Since 1977, I have worked as a stress management consultant to individuals, companies, and associates. The consistent stressor throughout these contacts with these people and organizations has been the stress around money and managing financial expectations. This book can offer the awareness of the problem and solutions that can help the motivated person take back some of the "control" that has slipped away.

The balance of mind/body/spirit is critical for health and happiness. *Mind Over Money* offers positive and direct suggestions to develop better balance of personal finance.

— L. John Mason, Ph.D., founder
of the Stress Education Center and
: *Reduction*
iving Life's

MIND OVER MONEY

Wayne E. Nance &
Edward A. Charlesworth, Ph.D.

Publishers Since 1798

THOMAS NELSON PUBLISHERS
Nashville

Published in Nashville, Tennessee, by Thomas Nelson, Inc.

Scripture quotations are from the NEW KING JAMES VER-SION of the Bible. Copyright © 1979, 1980, 1982, Thomas Nelson, Inc., Publishers.

Library of Congress Cataloging-in-Publication Data

Nance, Wayne E.
  Mind over money / Wayne E. Nance, Edward A. Charlesworth.
    p. cm.
  ISBN 0-8407-6743-0 (pb.)
  1. Finance, Personal.   2. Self-actualization (Psychology).
I. Charlesworth, Edward A., 1949– .   II. Title.
HG179.N354   1993
332.024—dc20   93-5694
                                                               CIP

Printed in the United States of America

1 2 3 4 5 6 7 - 98 97 96 95 94 93

For the love of money is a root of all kinds of evil, for which some have strayed from the faith in their greediness, and pierced themselves through with many sorrows.

1 Timothy 6:10

Dedication

I want to thank Shannon, Christel, Melissa, and Kara for their support over the past two years. Without the support of my family, this project could not have become a reality.

—Wayne Nance

I would like to dedicate this book to the loving memory of my parents, Albert Ernest and Wilma Nadine Charlesworth. My parents were models of fiscal responsibility, frugality, and life simplification. Upon executing their estate I discovered a system of organization and responsibility that I am still striving to duplicate.

—Ed Charlesworth

Acknowledgments

Many people have contributed to the final edition of this book. First we would like to thank our families for showing us patience, love, and encouragement. Throughout the long project they have helped us in many ways. Our wives have always been kind and supportive of our efforts to communicate those principles we believe.

Ronald Nathan, Ph.D., Dr. Charlesworth's co-author of *Stress Management: A Comprehensive Guide to Wellness*, has been a valuable colleague and friend.

Many of our clients and workshop attendees have brought us favorite quotes and vignettes on napkins and scraps of paper. To them we are deeply indebted, and to the possible authors of quotes whom we missed properly acknowledging, we sincerely apologize.

The 1980s brought economic booms and busts that shattered the illusions and dreams of many families and companies. Working intensely with these families and company executives has allowed us to begin understanding the importance of the old family values rooted in many of our spiritual backgrounds.

We would also like to acknowledge our friend Ron Haynes, who provided excellent guidance and encouragement.

We also thank countless other professionals, such as accountants, bookkeepers, and attorneys who have brought their expertise to bear on this project. Specifically, we want to thank Dwight Arnold, CPA, for his assistance with amortization tables.

Finally, thanks to Reggie Churchwell for believing in our project from the beginning and for introducing us to the Nashville area.

WHY DO WE FAIL FINANCIALLY?

1. Lack of financial training at home

2. Lack of financial education in schools

3. A biased commission sales system in the financial industry

4. Low self-esteem

5. Attempts to "buy" happiness

Contents

SECTION IV
Putting It All Together

APPENDICES

GLOSSARY

1. *Money Market*—An interest-bearing checking or savings account with no withdrawal penalties. Interest earned each 30-day period. The number of transactions per month can be limited.

2. *C.D. (certificate of deposit)*—An interest bearing account which has a 30-day, 60-day, 90-day, 180-day, 365-day, 5-year, etc. period of investment. An early withdrawal penalty is assessed if you pull money out prior to maturity.

3. *Annuity*—An insurance company's product that is comparable to a bank's C.D. A life insurance policy without a death benefit. Interest is paid on your principal for a period of time established by the company. Early withdrawal penalties apply during the first 5-15 years of the annuity depending on the company you choose.

4. *Mutual Funds*—Any investment pool of money managed by professional money managers in which the investor shares mutually with other investors in multiple investments within the fund.

5. *Life Insurance*—An insurance company product price based upon mortality cost, age, sex, health of the insured in which the insurance company pays a death benefit to the named beneficiary at the time of the insured's death.

6. *Stock*—ownership in the corporations of America.

7. *Bonds*—Lending of money to corporations, governments, and municipalities.

8. *Equity*—The accumulation of wealth within an investment. Equity is determined by taking present market value of an investment and subtracting any debt from the investment.

9. *Sales Charge*—A cost incurred when allowing an investment manager of money to manage your investment decisions. This charge can occur lump sum on the front or back end of an investment. It also can be assessed annually.

10. *Budget*—an organized method of keeping monthly and annual records of expenses incurred. It is a measurement which allows us to know where we have been and where we are able to go financially.

11. *Will*—A legal document which allows the distribution of one's property to their proper loved ones at the time of death. It also is an investment that will help some avoid settlement cost at death and allow the individual to name a guardian for their children.

12. *Long-term investment*—An investment period of time which is typically longer than 5 years.

13. *Short-term investment*—An investment period of time which is typically 1-5 years.

14. *Emergency Fund*—A savings account or money market account that is approximately 3 months of your budget needs.

15. *Retirement age*—Any age that an individual sees as a goal to *reduce* their needs to *work* and *increase* their time to *play*.

16. *I.R.A.*—Individual Retirement Account, for people who do not have a company sponsored retirement plan. The earnings are then deferred up to age 70 1/2. Early withdrawal penalties apply before age 59 1/2.

17. *401K Plan*—A company-sponsored retirement plan in which the company will typically match up to 50% of an employee's monthly contribution out of their paycheck. The employee's contribution is tax deductible and tax deferred annually into the investment choices of the employee. The amount of the company match and the vesting periods are at the discretion of each company.

18. *Vesting*—A period of years selected by an employer in which the employee must meet the years required in order to receive all of the retirement money placed into the employee account by the employer.

19. *Financial Statement*—A "score card" of how well a person is doing financially. This allows the individual to take the present value of assets and deduct the amount owed against them in order to let the individual and their lenders know the true "net" value of their various investments.

20. *Financial Cycle*—A cycle based upon the self-esteem of an individual developed from childhood as it relates to *money* and *spending habits.*

21. *Amortization*—A schedule of principal and interest payments on a mortgage which reflects the payoff balance from year to year.

22. *Term Life Insurance*—A life insurance policy that covers a specified period of time and then expires. As

the policyholder ages, either the premiums increase or the coverage decreases.

23. *Group Life Insurance*—A low-cost life insurance coverage provided by an employer for a group of employees. It typically terminates when the employee leaves the employer.

Foreword

The age of "new frugality" in the 1990's and beyond will demand our increasing attention to the relationship between financial matters and personal wellness. *Mind Over Money* effectively covers the financial waterfront—from the U.S. debt to family values to personal financial wellness. It describes in clear terms the dangers of leading financially unhealthy lifestyles and the importance of investing in our own future. As CEO of a large financial services and insurance company, I wholeheartedly agree. But perhaps equally important to our financial security is our own personal lifestyle and wellness choices. This is a good book for anyone interested in building financial, emotional, and physical wellness.

Unlike other books on financial planning, this book gives a balanced, meaningful view of the individual as a whole person—not just a money-making, asset-building machine. Nance and Charlesworth are right on target—building a healthy, meaningful, and secure future involves not only the marshalling and prudent investment of assets, but a choice of healthy lifestyles as well. *Mind Over Money* offers valuable advice for achieving these goals. May it bring you closer to your goal of personal financial wellness!

G. David Hurd
Chairman and CEO
The Principal Financial Group

SECTION I

Understanding Financial Dysfunction

CHAPTER ONE

The Molding of Dysfunctional Spending

For thus says the LORD: "You have sold yourselves for nothing, and you shall be redeemed without money."

Isaiah 52:3

— • • • —

"This desire for the rewards of the future . . . hastens us through our brief lives . . . and cheats us of all the spaciousness of time."

J. Mishan,
economist

— • • • —

Beware of little expenses; a small leak will sink a great ship.

Benjamin Franklin

— • • • —

The man who will live above his present circumstances, is in great danger of soon living beneath them; or as the Italian proverb says, "The man that lives by hope, will die by despair."

Joseph Addison

— • • • —

Angst in the Land of Opportunity

We are all searching for the American dream—endless opportunities and acquiring more than our parents. The pilgrims settled this country in search of freedom. Today we seem bound with iron chains to the fiscal lifestyle choices we make in the land of opportunity. America is a country full of two-income families and latchkey kids, but we still cannot keep up with our spending appetites. We have bought more "stuff," but the strangling chains of debt do not allow us to enjoy it.

The media bombards us with new products and "must-have" conveniences. Their strategies have produced a group of middle-class citizens striving for possessions never dreamed of by previous generations. Big-screen color televisions, computers, and fax machines are common in our homes and offices today. We find ourselves "living to work" and "working to live" while losing touch with true happiness and deep, satisfying relationships.

Our modern lives have become dysfunctional as we have sought to fulfill our parents' unfulfilled dreams and "keep up with the Joneses." We have followed subliminally programmed values from the media and from advertisers, and allowed others to define our sense of purpose. Our forefathers had meaningful lives trying to establish a country where they could develop industries and live free of religious persecution. We now seem to have lost sight of the sources of true happiness. We no longer feel that we are important as individuals and that what we do matters. More and more people are just living day to day, with "too much month at the end of the money."

— • • • —

"Advertising may be described as the science of arresting the human intelligence long enough to get money from it."

Stephen Butler Leacock,
Canadian humorist and economist

• • •

We strive; we struggle; we sacrifice—all for money. In our striving we are also slipping ever deeper into a quagmire of dissatisfaction and debt. Our lives have become dysfunctional and our hearts heavy. Perhaps now is the time to reevaluate both our lives and our lifestyles. We need to determine what gives us purpose and fulfillment and tailor our lifestyles to be natural extensions of those deep desires.

• • •

"America is a country that doesn't know where it is going but is determined to set a speed record getting there."

Laurence J. Peter

• • •

"Lifestyles of the Rich and Famous," or Sick Lifestyles, Bodies, Minds, and Spirits?

We are exposed to the lifestyles of the so-called "rich and famous" through our televisions and tabloids. We see the power and wealth of the Ewings of "Dallas" and the Carringtons of "Dynasty." We were raised to expect the best and have the most. We believe that "time is money," and that we can "think and grow rich." Our tapes and televisions try to teach us the "psychology of success" and how to "make a fortune in real estate with no money down." With all these influences, is it any wonder that our debts continue to grow and that we continue to live financially dysfunctional lifestyles?

THE DYSFUNCTIONAL FINANCIAL LIFESTYLE

A dysfunctional financial lifestyle is an addictive and malignant pattern of consumption, purchasing, spending, or deferred payment for current lifestyle choices in any person, including those of average intelligence, morals, and personality, based on preconscious beliefs that

- more "stuff" is always better
- designer, highly visible, or advertised items yield more statisfaction
- the most technologically advanced version of fax, beeper, mobile phone, stereo, or large-screen television reflects that we have "made it" and are therefore worthwhile
- what the "Joneses" have should be pursued since we are as worthy as they are
- if we have the "right" clothes, cars, houses, watches, or pens in life, we will be accepted and held in high esteem by our peers
- "he who dies with the most toys wins" in the game of life
- "time is money"
- material or financial desires are infinite; people must relentlessly pursue "the petty pot of gold at the end of the plastic rainbow"
- if our income does not keep pace with our desires, we should tranquilize our anxious dysphoria with the American drug of choice and follow the wisdom of the great leaders of our deficit-spending society to $charge$ our way out of despair.

—Wayne Nance and
Ed Charlesworth

The "Yuppies" Become "Grumpies"

The 1980s in the United States spawned the notorious "Yuppies" or Young Urban Professionals who sought expensive cars, second homes, and flaunted their symbols of success. The Yuppies keep a consumer society buzzing. Consume. Consume. Consume.

The 1990s through the foreseeable future will bring the downsizing of business and lower consumer expectations, resulting in profound social and psychological change. This change is giving birth to "Grumpies" or Grown-Up Mature Professionals. This population is less concerned about material status symbols and more concerned about the environment, health, spiritual peace, their children's education, leisure time, and their own retirement. They have learned you can have many "toys" and no time to play with them. They have learned that "stuff" requires maintenance, breaks down, gets stolen, and may bring little satisfaction after the initial challenge of acquisition has been fulfilled.

The New Frugality

We are entering an age of "new frugality." The boom years are over. We are shackled with debt individually and nationally, our confidence is down, and no political rhetoric will undo our concern about the well-being of our future generations. Small businesses and major corporations are becoming "leaner and meaner" as they scale down through attrition, early retirements, layoffs, and decreased benefits.

In the 1980s a hospital could get away with charging exorbitant sums without scrutiny because "insurance paid for it." For example, a bottle of hydrogen peroxide could be purchased at a discount pharmacy for $.33 A hospital charged $18.00 for the same bottle. Even if the hospital bought it for retail, that is a markup of 5,500 percent. But the days of "who cares, the insurance pays for it" are rapidly ending. More and more people of the "new frugality" will learn how to read the bills and ask about charges before just taking whatever they are given. Many middle-class Americans are unable to afford medical insurance, even less expensive plans which have high co-payments and deductibles. About 55 percent of America's largest corporations now require employees to pay a portion of their health insurance, up from 41 percent in 1986. For the first time in its recent history, one of America's leading car manufacturers does not have free medical benefits for all employees. Why? Because their annual health care bill exceeds $3.4 billion—$900 per car or truck sold in the United States each year.

Although professional sports figures continue to command exorbitant salaries, there is a growing resentment that will eventually show up at the box office and later in the contracts. One professional football team is being sued for its policy of blacking out all home games that are not sold out. The person suing the team is an elderly, homebound lady who cannot go to the games for medical reasons and feels deprived of the opportunity to support her hometown team. It reminds us of the times we could watch championship boxing matches on regular television without paying a special $40 cable fee.

We believe the underlying psychology of the 1980s was "charge what the market can bear" and "I deserve to have 'things' as much as he does." The underlying psychology of the 1990s will be "patronize those who are fair" and "neither he nor I deserve to have so much, to indenture future generations, or to be ecologically irresponsible." The live-for-today policies and politics violate basic moral values and traditions that could provide our children's children with a better world. The dominant themes for the 75 million baby boomers born between 1946 and 1964 will be a more traditional family value system, raising children, and an instinctual and atavistic effort to promote survival of the species and world.

— • • • —

The most affluent faction of the nation's 75 million baby boomers is cutting back on conspicuous consumption and thinking more about saving for the future.

Associated Press

— • • • —

Are We Planting Trees for Our Grandchildren?

We once heard the story of a traveler who came upon an old man planting a tree. When the traveler asked when the tree would produce fruit, the old man replied "70 years or so." The traveler looked at the man in disbelief and asked if the old man really expected to live that long. The reply was, "No, but I did not find the world bare when I entered it, and since my fathers before me planted for when I was born, so do I plant for those who will come after me."

— • • • —

Even if I knew with certainty that the world would end tomorrow, I would plant a tree today.

Martin Luther King, Jr.

— • • • —

CHAPTER TWO

The Psychology of Financial Dysfunction

Parable of the Talents

For the kingdom of heaven is like a man traveling to a far country, who called his own servants and delivered his goods to them. And to one he gave five talents, to another two, and to another one, to each according to his own ability; and immediately he went on a journey. Then he who had received the five talents went and traded with them, and made another five talents. And likewise he who had received two gained two more also. But he who had received one went and dug in the ground, and hid his lord's money.

Matthew 25:14-18

• • •

We Have Measured by False Standards

Our dysfunctional financial lifestyles have steered us away from planting for the future and have led us down the paths of immediate gratification, short-term gains, and the illusion of success. During the 1980s, heavy spending and borrowing at the government, corporate, and individual levels created a false prosperity. Unfortunately the cost for this false prosperity will have to be paid by us and future generations. Powerful influences have been eroding our better judgment and turning us toward the short-sighted, narrow-minded pursuit of only living for today.

• • •

> *Men measure by the false standards that everyone seeks power, success, riches for himself and admires others who attain them while undervaluing the truly precious things in life.*
>
> Sigmund Freud

• • •

"Three-Car Garage, and Still Adding On"

Before Waylon and Willie and the boys decided to get back to the basics in life, they were pursuing the three-car garage, and still adding on. These compulsions have become stereotyped recurring acts and rituals for most of the country. We often feel an irresistible urge to buy something new, add on to the house, or in some other way spend money to quiet our existential misery. Marvin Drellich states in the *American Handbook of Psychiatry* that "Anxiety is felt if the compulsion is not performed, and temporary relief of anxiety occurs when the act is carried out in the 'proper' fashion." In America we certainly try to carry out our compulsive spending in the "proper" way.

Spending compulsions serve as a defense mechanism to channel our energies into "approved," outwardly harmless activities. This prevents the awareness of our underlying angst, anger, emotional confusion, social isolation, low self-esteem, and sense of desperation. Initially, the compulsive act of spending may be paired with a desire to resist the compulsion, but soon there is a sense of mounting tension. Giving in to the compulsion can provide a release from the tension, albeit a temporary and short-lived relief. With repeated failure to resist the compulsion, we begin to give in to it more quickly, spending money without the desire to resist the urge to shop.

Compulsive spending occurs as a way to prevent or neutralize our pain. Unfortunately, this compulsive act is often not realistically connected to the true source of our pain. For example, buying a new car does not heal our deep, underlying feelings of poor self-esteem. Owning the latest high-tech gadget does not truly satisfy our basic need for emotional closeness. And wearing designer clothes does not hide us from our true selves or from feelings of purposelessness. But still we try, and still we buy.

In counseling thousands of clients and investors over the years, we have observed the consistent, prevailing issue of *wanting more and more and not knowing when enough is enough.* Along these lines, Guy Clark wrote a song which says "too much just ain't enough." That certainly sums up how our compulsive spending "just ain't enough" to really make us happy.

The act of spending money alters our consciousness into believing we are in a *comfort zone.* Unfortunately, since this *comfort zone* is an illusion, we must drink or take more of our drug of choice to avoid the *discomfort zone* of reality. So, compulsive spending can be equated with the alcoholic's nectar which temporarily shelters us from our pain, only to poison our bodies, minds, and spirits in the long run. Eventually, the dripping faucet of perpetual spending depletes our souls, leaving us thirsting for a real sense of purpose in life, other than to merely survive until the next payday.

———•••———

Money is not required to buy one necessity of the soul.

Henry David Thoreau

———•••———

He's a Twenty-four-Carat Gold **Spendaholic,** Living on Forty Proof "It's OK"

Our spending habits can help us dig a financial grave. We, the authors, call these habits *Spendaholism.* Conspicuous consumption becomes the drug of choice for those who cannot control their emotions without going to the charge card or revolving credit line for immediate and temporary gratification. They may know they are overextended, but still they say, "It's OK. I can charge it."

Spending can easily become a form of entertainment. Like the alcoholic in denial who says he or she can quit anytime, the Spendaholic feels the same way. The *foodaholic* may stop at a $3.95 all-you-can-eat buffet, while the Spendaholic will not miss the close-out "Midnight Madness Sale" at the local wholesale warehouse to spend massive amounts of money ... because of saving so much!

Spendaholism usually starts out very innocently, but quickly becomes a way of life. It is easy to fall into the "got-to-have-the-best-of-everything" syndrome, which fuels the Spendaholic dilemma. Now we are not just spending, we are breaking the bank by having excessive charge purchases.

———•••———

Some debts are fun when you are acquiring them, but
none are fun when you set about retiring them.

Ogden Nash

• • •

"False Prosperity"

One major financial dilemma in the United States is how many of us drain our physical energy trying to achieve a "false prosperity," which saps our emotional energy for meaningful marital and family time.

With the best of intentions, we give money out to our kids like candy so they can have a good time. We strive to give them everything their hearts desire. Before we know it, designer jeans and new sports cars become surrogate parents. Then, a nagging guilt eats away at us, and a chronic boredom pervades our children.

This false prosperity has led both the parents and the children to forget what it is to truly enjoy each other. And neither knows how to escape the web that has been woven.

This false prosperity may even lead us to seek ways to deny the reality of how out of balance our lives have become. We may wake up only to find that we are unable to connect emotionally with our children, just as Harry Chapin sang about in his song "Cat's in the Cradle." We may then ask our children when they are coming home to visit only to hear them reply "we'll get together soon." But we know all too well that soon may rarely come.

• • •

Lots of fellows think a home is only good to borrow money on.

Kin Hubbard,
American cartoonist

———•·•·•———

The Ideal Versus the Real

Two major forces have collided. One is the expectation of what life should be. This includes the role models on which some of us were raised, which came from television shows: "Ozzie and Harriet," "Father Knows Best," "Leave It to Beaver," and "The Donna Reed Show." In these shows Father came home early and spent time with his family. Mother stayed at home and baked cookies for her children's after-school snack. The children were not bombarded with major moral dilemmas with which to cope; problems could easily be worked out in thirty minutes, air time, including commercials. Then we began to question that this may be reality for everyone else, but we, personally, were failing miserably to meet these expectations.

The other major force is the reality of what life *is*—an achiever society where quality of life is sacrificed for "doing better than my parents did." Doing better has often become equated with having more stuff and less time.

We now have as the norm a two-income family, but we tell ourselves it is out of necessity. We have more cars and more microwaves, more portable and extension telephones to save us steps, and more services such as call waiting, call forwarding, three-way calling, conference calling, modems, faxes, and personal "800" numbers. We may not know how to use all these features, but we have them anyway. We also have video recorders, though most of us have a hard time programming them. Half the time they blink, telling us it is twelve o'clock when it isn't.

— • • • —

Wealth is not his that has it, but his that enjoys it.
Benjamin Franklin

— • • • —

The children in many financially "successful" homes are finding that money takes the place of love and family time. This was never meant to happen, yet perfectly good people have become victims of our consumer society. Once these dysfunctional habits are learned, the teaching may be passed from generation to generation. Parents want their children to have everything they did not have; therefore, children are receiving more and more stuff.

Children, in many cases, feel insecure about their relationships with their parents but have learned that, whatever the deficiency in life may be, spending money and buying toys will solve their problems.

— • • • —

"Keeping Up with the Joneses"

In our financial society, families are set up to fail. This is due to false teachings that reinforce poor habits for generations. What we eat, the clothes we buy, our taste in cars are influenced greatly by our families. The "Joneses" in America are often our idols, and it is extremely gratifying to amplify our sense of false importance by elevating ourselves to their level. The truth is that many of the "Joneses" are overextended on multiple credit cards, late with the Mercedes payment, and paying the children's orthodontist on an installment plan.

———•••———

Do not accustom yourself to consider debt only as an inconvenience; you will find it a calamity.
Samuel Johnson

———•••———

The Financial Merry-Go-Round

We are caught upon the carousel of time. People go round and round in life's financial cycle. Many people said twenty years ago, they were running close financially, a little short on cash, or that next month things will be better. It is unfortunate, but in many families where financial devastation takes place over and over again, the family predicts that they are going to get on their feet after Christmas, tax time, summer vacations, or when school starts. They are getting ready to commence, to begin, to start their new financial game plan. It's much like starting a new diet. When is the best time to begin a diet? Well, many of these people are in the same shape today, or worse.

The financial problems that occur in American homes today are brought about by different factors. In many cases, parents are unable to teach children about money because dysfunctional financial teachings have carried forward three to five generations. If this is not enough deficiency, the school systems in our country have too few educational programs to teach children how to deal with the financial decisions that will face them in life. When Dr. Charlesworth finished nine years of college, one year internship, and one year post-doctoral fellowship, he had received absolutely no training in how to plan and manage the fiscal side of practicing psychology. Our nation itself does not model fiscal responsibility.

———•••———

The American consumer: Someone who knows the cost of everything, but the value of nothing.

———•••———

Are We Planning to Fail, or Failing to Plan?

Based on numerous studies and affirmed by Mr. Nance's years of experience as a financial consultant, approximately 90 percent of all American families experience financial distress during their working years or after retirement. Although the causes are varied, the most significant reason is failure to implement a prudent plan to use our available resources. Instead we seek pleasure through our spending habits, put off important decisions until tomorrow, compulsively overspend for immediate gratification, fail to prepare for emergencies, become disabled, or prematurely die.

Our society is propelling itself into a future of indentured servitude because of its current deficit spending choices. The balancing of budgets has been blasted into Tomorrowland, with no sense of how current decisions will influence the future.

Good News, Bad News

We have learned to spend and consume, but we have not learned to save. The good news is that the "new frugality" suggests the emergence of an underlying maturity and psychological development, away from the narcissistically driven "me, me, me" generation toward a generation which holds the high ideals and values that made this country great. The bad news is that we have created a hungry, overweight beast that, in order to slim down, will have to go through withdrawal, fiscal gnashing of teeth, and cries of "unfair" and "you can't do that to me." You can't just send a third or fourth family member out to work in order to feed the beast, and yet the economy actually needs more spending to force it out of the economic doldrums of supply and demand. The price for *financial wellness* will not be cheap, yet the price of not seeking a better balance would be a travesty to future generations.

The Costs of Dysfunctional Financial Lifestyles

Obsessive spending, excessive debt, and financial mismanagement are creating sick people—people who are depressed, anxious, unhappy. Medical costs continue to increase yearly, and many families can no longer afford to pay health insurance premiums. The largest single supplier to General Motors is an insurance company. In one state, three out of four marriages end in divorce. For both men and women, the most frequently given reason for marital stress is "money." Twenty percent of all American children live in poverty, the highest percentage of poverty of any age group. The number of children living with their parents has declined; now over six million children live with other relatives, neighbors, family friends, or in institutions.

These are high prices to pay for dysfunctional financial lifestyles.

———•••———

I know well what I am fleeing from, but not what I am in search of.

Michel de Montaigne

———•••———

You Only Go Around Once, So Grab for All the Gusto

Western liberalism has favored democratic reforms, civil liberties, and the use of public resources to promote social progress. Descartes founded modern philosophy with his famous principle, "I think, therefore I am." In essence he divided the world into the thinking mind and the inert. Rational thought has led to science and technology unheard of before our modern generations. We have harnessed the stars and the atom, the rivers and the winds. The Western philosophy that says man may master nature and that "you only go around once in life, so you've got to grab for all the gusto" has helped us advance, but it has also helped us lose sight of some truly important things in life. Unfortunately, our narcissistic placement of man above all else has led to widespread destruction of non-human life and the very environment that we as humans depend on for our own existence. We are spiritually poorer, and all of our financial grabbing "for all the gusto" has not quieted our inner turmoil or brought us closer to a contented life.

There seems to be a modern ethic which affirms individualism as the absolute value. We believe that thought has reached its limit.

Our bodies, minds, and spirits are breaking down in response to our lifestyles. Our lives are full, but are they full of what we truly need?

• • •

In our culture we make heroes of the men who sit on top of a heap of money.

Max Lerner,
American scientist

• • •

CHAPTER THREE

The Spirit of Money

Money does all things for reward. Some are pious and honest as long as they thrive upon it, but if the devil himself gives better wages, they soon change their party.

Seneca

• • •

Ho! Everyone who thirsts, come to the waters; and you who have no money, come, buy and eat. Yes, come, buy wine and milk without money and without price.

Isaiah 55:1

• • •

In the Eyes of Advertisers, We Are Not All Created Equal

In the eyes of God we are all equal. But, unfortunately, in the eyes of advertisers and salespeople we are not. They work hard to qualify buyers so as not to waste time on those who do not have the financial means to buy the latest product, gimmick, or gadget. We should not be measured by our balance sheets, bank balance, or income level, but we often are. We may lose our way, in terms of what is really important in life, if we get too tied up to the material world and forget the spiritual side of our life.

Do Our Lifestyles Leave Us Spiritually Spent?

Spirituality is the foundation for living a balanced life. Today's homes are often lacking in the traditional family and spiritual values that made America a great financial power in the world. A strong home life for this nation's children once meant personal values and the good old, red-blooded American traditions of honesty, hard work, unselfishness, and belief in God. Perhaps as we reflect on the dysfunctional lifestyles of the 1990s, we may begin to appreciate the value of clichés about God, the flag, and apple pie.

Home, in today's society, is often a place where either one parent or both parents are so busy working to make ends meet that they have limited time to spend with the children. We seem to have little time to spend nurturing our spiritual needs. We are emotionally drained from pursuing the dollar. Out of balance with our own values. Lost as to how to fill up our empty souls. So, we buy gifts, videos, designer jeans to communicate to our children and family that we love them. Since this stuff costs money, we have to work longer to pay the bills. Since we are working longer, we feel more dysphoria and guilt. So, we buy *more* stuff. And on and on it goes.

This cycle has the inadvertent result of teaching our children to value stuff over the substance and essence of life that makes it truly worth living. It is often too late when we discover that our children or spouse really didn't want the stuff, but wanted the love, listening, and warmth that we failed to bring home.

Symbols of Success,
Instead of Spiritual Sustenance

Many of us are so wrapped up in our jobs, golf games, community organizations, and political offices that we are forgetting where our priorities are. Our children's spiritual values, self-esteem, and self-worth are developed in the home. But many of our children are missing this development and fall victim to gangs, drugs, alcohol, and violence. Gangs kill and rob for the material symbols of success, such as jackets, jewelry, which are often only substitutes for the acceptance and love they're not receiving at home. Instead of a nurturing atmosphere, we give empty symbols of nurturance through the things that money can buy. But the symbols are not enough.

The personal value systems that are being taught to our children through the news media, television, videos, and movies are often not what we really want them to learn. The days of looking up to movie stars, ball players, and personal heroes seem lost at times. Children today have heroes who often endorse items only for the money and flaunt their material possessions with little regard for promoting the values our children need to live fully balanced, happy lives. So, who will teach our kids values? Much is being left to the schools, and the rest is gladly championed by advertisers, marketers, media, and movie makers, all who have their own personal financial interests in mind. We must get back to basics and teach kids what personal values are all about. It must be done by the example of our lifestyle and quality of time we spend with them.

We live in a "me" world where such things as money, power, possessions, and personal gain are often put ahead of other personal traits. In our "me" society most of us may get lost and believe that money buys us happiness. It's important to remember that God gave us the potential for a fulfilling life with or without wealth and designer clothes. We came into this world with nothing and we'll leave with nothing. All that remains will be the images of the way we lived our life. *If we help those who are in need, we will be blessed many times over in ways we could never imagine. We are also charged with the responsibility of teaching these lasting values to our children and making sure they understand that helping others is not just a God-given ability, but is a way to true happiness and contentment.* When the narcissistically driven "me" generation turns from pursuing objects through deficit spending to devoting the "me" to serve people in spiritually meaningful and productive ways, then financial dysfunction will fade.

If You Are Spiritually Spent, You May Feel an "Entitled Demanding"

The work ethic in this country has deteriorated in the past decades as we have become a society of entitlement programs. One psychological characteristic of a particular personality disorder is a sense of "entitled demanding"—"I demand to have more and more material possessions and free handouts, and I'm entitled to it." Families are sometimes taught through television and video that it's cool to avoid work and find the easy way to beat the system. As parents, we sometimes give our children everything they want so they will have it better than we did. This is often a way of avoiding our own guilt for feeling emotionally in pain, spiritually spent, and not wanting to deal with the inconvenience caused by setting boundaries. We feel guilty because we do not spend quality or quantity time with our children, so we let them have what they want without their working for it. We "buy them," so to speak. And they grow up knowing that if they flunk out of school or get fired from work, they will still have Mom and Dad to run to.

In most cases, we are given a mind and a healthy body to be a productive citizen. We therefore have a responsibility to teach our children that a hard day's work yields a fair day's wage.

Many of us think that wearing out a church pew is equal to being a Christian and a very spiritual person. Not so. If we are at the church every time the doors open but are not fulfilling our responsibilities to God, our families and our fellow men, then we must look at our spirituality and re-examine our direction. God honors hard work, perserverance, and faithfulness.

How the Denial of Our Feelings and Spiritual Needs Leads to Financial Dysfunction

We live in a country where people are dealing daily with spiritual emptiness, fear, anger, guilt, and mistrust. Many of us may also feel a sense of financial hopelessness.

Many of our feelings are developed early in childhood and may contribute to our joy or misery throughout life's journey. Sometimes we "stuff" our feelings or ignore our spiritual needs. "Stuffing" is when you cram a thirty-six-inch ball of emotion into a twelve-inch hiding place and pretend that it will not ooze into the subconscious issues of our human relationships. Not meeting our spiritual needs and stuffing feelings can lead to addictions or compulsive habits that may change from time to time. And without true awareness of our inner pain, we never seem to conquer these dysfunctional habits.

Just as a foodaholic or alcoholic may use denial, so the Spendaholic may deny that his or her compulsive spending is really a pleasurable act meant to cover inner feelings of loneliness, anger, sadness, depression, or spiritual distress. The feeling of enjoying the spending of money and charging credit cards to acquire possessions creates the illusion of being happy and in charge of our life.

Self-denial is a problem common to us all. But it is impossible for us to change our lives and the way we react to life's challenges if we do not first admit that something needs to be changed. Denial hinders change.

If You Don't Think It's "Broke," You Can't Fix It

Why do we deny?

We deny because if we acknowledge to ourselves and others that we have a problem, we seem to become less than "normal" (whatever "normal" is). We also deny because admission can lead to an inner tension to become accountable for our actions and to work on resolving the problem. Since we often feel helpless to change, or have already tried and failed, denial allows us to temporarily avoid the pain of confronting ourselves and our problem.

When we choose to become accountable for our behavior, we may turn to another for help. Who might that other be? It could be our best friend, our spouse, our minister, our work associate, or our counselor. Often, in order to overcome denial, we must be able to confront ourselves as we really are, with all our foibles, faults, and imperfections. All of us should turn to our spiritual side of life in order to do this. We should turn to God for acceptance and unconditional love. Once we surrender to him, we can then follow a lifelong path in which our pain, loneliness, sorrow, and guilt can be confronted.

It is difficult for us to stop and look at ourselves as we pass the "mirrors of life." We see what we want to see, and we imagine we are who we want to be. It's easy to blame our shortcomings on others—our childhood, our family, our society—because this frees us from the responsibility of our lives and our actions. We may sometimes feel discouraged and perpetuate our dysfunctional habits of excess spending, eating, or drinking and think to ourselves, "That's just the way it is."

For most people, a spiritual lifestyle is difficult to maintain in a "me" society where the emphasis is on grabbing the gusto. We think we don't need any help. Unfortunately, this false belief can blind us to our spiritual needs and to the truth that our many purchases will not fill the void in our souls.

The Spiritual Side of Finding Financial Wellness

Change of habits or addictions must take place for us to improve our lifestyle. How does this change take place? For many of us to make these changes it is necessary to quiet ourselves in prayerful meditation and ask God for help and direction.

We may sometimes fail at conquering compulsive spending habits; but, remember, we must crawl before we can walk. Recognizing our problems, and being willing to work on them an inch at a time, is 90 percent of the battle. We can enjoy a more balanced financial life, but balancing our spiritual life along the way makes the changes lasting and worthy of a lifetime.

* * *

But Peter said to him, "Your money perish with you, because you thought that the gift of God could be purchased with money!"

Acts 8:20

CHAPTER FOUR

Uncle Sam's Dysfunctional Financial Lifestyle

And to preserve their independence, we must not let our rulers load us with perpetual debt. We must make our election between economy and liberty, or profusion and servitude.

Thomas Jefferson

• • •

Our Uncle's Own Dysfunctional Financial Lifestyle

Part of our dysfunctional lifestyle comes from the role model of our own Uncle Sam. From our government we have learned that spending our children's money is OK. We have shackled future generations with a $4 trillion ($4,000,000,000,000) federal debt, to which our leaders add nearly $1 billion dollars in new debt *every day*. In order not to have a deficit this year, we would have to double everyone's income taxes. That would not begin to pay off the national debt, but would only stop adding to it. Today, all the income taxes collected from the states west of the Mississippi go to just paying the interest on our debt. We pay over $214 billion per year just in interest.

• • •

Debt is the fatal disease of republics, the first thing and the mightiest to undermine governments and corrupt the people.

Wendell Phillips,
U.S. abolitionist/social reformer

• • •

Why You Should Be Concerned about the Federal Deficit

As a citizen of the United States, you pay a high price for the government deficit. The government must borrow money to live in deficit spending cycles, and this places it in competition with you for loans. It is estimated that every loan made to a consumer is two percentage points higher just because the greater demand for loans encourages lenders to raise interest rates.

When you have to pay more money in interest, you have less money to save, invest, or keep the consumer society going through purchases and spending. The same is true for employers and businesses. Consequently, they do not upgrade equipment which would allow workers to be more productive. And wages do not go up. When you are less productive and have less to spend, then the economy does not grow. If the economy does not grow, then tax revenues shrink. So the government has to raise your taxes or cut spending or borrow money; therefore, the cycle of deficit spending continues until interest rates go up further. Then hyperinflation occurs, and living standards fall.

————•••————

I place economy among the first and most important virtues, and public debt as the greatest of dangers . . . We must make our choice between economy and liberty, or profusion and servitude. If we can prevent the government from wasting the labors of the people under the pretense of caring for them, they will be happy.

Thomas Jefferson

————•••————

The State of Working America

In a recent study, the Economic Policy Institute reported that the average wages for blue-collar and white-collar workers has fallen about 12.4 percent over the last 15 years. The wage gap between men and women is declining—because of falling income for men, not because women are doing better. Industries are faced with increased competition from abroad and are taking cost-cutting measures to stay afloat. Income for the richest 1 percent of Americans grew during the last decade by almost 63 percent. However, for the bottom 60 percent of American families, incomes declined during the same period. The economy is failing most Americans, and we are in a long-term erosion of incomes and opportunities. There is falling confidence in America, and realization that future generations will not fare as well as their parents.

Are We Investing in Our Future?

Research and development funds in academic, corporate, and scientific pursuits for new and improved technology have fallen 2 to 3 percent per year since 1986. Education and achievement scores have dropped, and we have failed to educate our workers to be more efficient and productive. In a poll of employers, the Committee for Economic Development found that only 30 percent of students were adequately prepared to hold jobs in their businesses. Our real income has declined even though it has been masked by two-income households.

— • • —

Americanism means the virtues of courage, honor, justice, truth, sincerity, and hardihood—the virtues that made America. The things that will destroy America are prosperity-at-any-price, peace-at-any-price, safety-first instead of duty-first, the love of soft living and the get-rich-quick theory of life.

Theodore Roosevelt

— • • —

The U.S. Index of Social Health

For over twenty years, Fordham University professor Marc Miringoff has been tracking how our country is doing in terms of poverty, infant mortality, child abuse, teen suicide, drug abuse, school dropouts, unemployment, earnings, housing, health care costs, and crime. He has found that we are at the lowest point since the information has been analyzed: a score of only 42 out of a possible 100 points on the Index of Social Health. Professor Miringoff says, "There are many signs we have lost our sense of public concern."

The gap between the rich and the poor has broadened, and the number of children living in poverty has increased 33 percent. Out of sixteen problems being examined, six are now at the lowest point ever.

— • • • —

Economy is for the poor; the rich may dispense with it.

Christian Nestell Bovee

— • • • —

If I Offer You $15 Billion, Why Won't You Take It?

The United States government hires at great expense thousands of people to find waste and mismanagement. In a recent report, our auditors made recommendations, to the twenty largest federal agencies, that would have saved taxpayers $15 billion in waste. The agencies failed to follow these recommendations. Why?

The reason is this: We have a system of laws and regulations geared to uncover wasteful spending, but we lack a system to stop the waste. Agencies have little incentive to stop waste since future congressional funding is often based on how much is currently being spent. The Congress and the president are in charge of stopping waste, but taking away dollars disturbs constituents and special interest groups. Only until the voters demand more accountability will the waste stop. (Be a voter!)

— • • • —

No gain is so certain as that which proceeds from the economical use of what you already have.

Latin Proverb

— • • • —

The Erosion of Trust

We have developed our distorted fiscal system to the point that often criminals have more rights than their victims. Young children lose parents at the hands of murderers and drunk drivers. They will forever be affected by their losses, and yet the criminals are often set free, pay little restitution, and show no remorse. Usually criminals have little money to pay damages, and victims have little recourse.

On the other hand, if there is money to be made from litigation, it will probably be made. We cannot trust our legal system to protect us—the average citizen—yet litigation of lawsuits has become a $300 billion annual drag on the economy. Plaintiffs are recruited by trial lawyers through distasteful television advertising directed toward industries where big-dollar suits can be filed (for example, breast implants, railroad, shipping, auto accidents, workmen's comp, asbestos). Even if the plaintiff has no health impairment, he or she can still serve as a vehicle for litigation. Of the $9 billion dollars collected from the asbestos industry alone, approximately $6 billion has gone to lawyers. That same money could have created 200,000 jobs or 90,000 housing units.

Juries are growing tired of the inflated expenses of lawsuit judgments and will soon start capping the awards. They will turn against the lawyers who bring frivolous suits to secure lucrative out-of-court settlements. In one recent case, the victim walked away with $27,000 out of a $500,000 settlement. The lawyers received over $200,000, and the rest went to court costs and other expenses.

If you are the average hardworking, middle-class citizen, you probably have insurance for your house, health, automobile, and accidents. Did you know that you pay over 30 percent more for insurance because so many lawsuits occur?

White-collar criminals are also among us. Our banking institutions fail before our eyes, and we are asked to pay the bill. Retirement funds become worthless, while those veterans who built this country watch their life savings disappear. Our political leaders have more perquisites than we ever dreamed of having; and if they overspend, it's not a problem since their checks cannot bounce. Our scientists are caught faking data and stealing the credit for who discovered certain exotic diseases. From the pressure of "publish or perish," we have created both an erosion of excellence and ethics.

Yes, it's difficult to trust in the face of so many injustices.

The first stage of successful infant development is the establishment of trust. Can we teach our children this when we as adults have come to doubt it ourselves?

———•••———

Then Judias Iscariot, one of the twelve, went to the chief priests to betray Him to them. So when they heard it, they were glad, and promised to give him money. So he sought how he might conveniently betray Him.

Mark 14:10-11

———•••———

CHAPTER FIVE

The Many Faces of Financial Dysfunction

"Go your way; behold, I send you out as lambs among wolves. Carry neither money bag, sack, nor sandals; and greet no one along the road."

Luke 10:3-4

———•••———

The Financial Pathology of Everyday Living

When we think about ourselves, our friends and families, and the people whom we counsel on a daily basis, we become aware that most of us do not *plan* to experience chronic financial distress. What we become profoundly aware of is that most of us have strong moral values, are reasonably intelligent, motivated, and have good qualities of character. Why then are so many of us experiencing stress related to money?

Sometimes we are cast abruptly into financial stress because we failed to anticipate traumatic life events such as divorce, death, disability, and disease. A family can lose its primary wage earner through death, prolonged illness, or physical disability. Sometimes we slowly dig our own financial graves when we become addicted to dysfunctional financial lifestyles.

We probably did not start out intending to indulge bad spending habits that would lead us to work or worry our health and life away. But, along the way, we somehow got addicted to the goal of having more than our parents did. We somehow came to believe that self-esteem comes from what you possess. We believed the advertising propaganda that dictates we need certain clothes, cosmetics, or chemicals to be pretty, sexy, handsome, worthwhile.

Even our religious leaders are not immune to the addiction of a dysfunctional financial lifestyle. Money and materialism can topple religious empires, sending their once respected leaders to jail.

The effects of a dysfunctional financial lifestyle are not just an individual's problem. The sources and synergism are much greater than the individuals who make up this great country. The very essence of our leadership is addicted to the dysfunctional financial lifestyle. Even when we "read their lips," they fail to live up to their promises to stop the financial bloodletting. The federal debt continues to escalate because our leaders are addicted to living in deficit. Perhaps we need to question a lifestyle that attempts to satisfy itself through the philosophy of Artemus Ward:

> *Let us all be happy and live within our means, even if we have to borrow money to do it with.*

* * *

One Throw Away from Life's Reality

On a recent trip to Las Vegas, it became apparent how addictive dysfunctional spending is the cornerstone of one of the world's greatest resorts. People from around the world flock to Las Vegas to spend hours and hours in this adult Disneyland of gambling. Here you see everything from wealthy high rollers to ordinary peole seeking to control their own personal row of slot machines.

People spend hours leaning over the crap tables and sitting at the baccarat and blackjack tables. They sit with cigarette in hand, drinking Scotch and water. They throw the dice and chips like inexpensive toys, while waiting to feast at the $3.95 buffet where they can eat themselves into oblivion.

While standing in line for the $3.95 buffet they will put dollar after dollar into the $1.00, one-armed bandit just outside the restaurant. While in the restaurant, they will steadily place their keno bets at $5.00 a pop. Feverishly, they rush through their meal in order to get back to their chosen game of chance.

In Las Vegas you can double up your bets to get back your losses from the previous hour. Even though your dealer is winning for the house, you just *know* that if you will only hang on long enough the table will turn and you will become a winner. You start out the day on adrenaline and excitement from the anticipation of the win; but as reality sets in, you become dismayed and fatigued. If only you could hit the big one a couple times, everything would be OK; you could get back to even. You take what is left and throw it all out there, because you're sure to win now; the odds are in your favor since you've failed so many times so far. Your ego does not want you to leave as a loser, even though the real issue may be that you've already spent next month's rent, grocery money, or car payment.

Las Vegas can teach us a lot about life and the addictive personalities we possess. If we have no strategy or backup plan and feel we can simply live our financial life a day at a time, we may believe that gambling will pay off for us in the long run. In reality 21, 7, or 11 will not come up very often, but we sometimes hope it will happen enough to get us by. If it doesn't, the government, a friend, a family member, or our children will bail us out, right? Meanwhile, we may bury our insecurities about money in food, drugs, alcohol, or charge cards, which only compounds our addictive processes.

Las Vegas is in Nevada, but it is open daily in many of our personal lives. We all want instant financial gains with little effort. We believe that there is an adult Disneyland that will create a Peter Pan ride for us through life.

— • • • —

The safest way to double your money is to fold it over once and put it in your pocket.

Kin Hubbard,
American cartoonist

— • • • —

Women and Financial Literacy

The evidence that women are extremely vulnerable to financial dysfunction is convincing. Male mates typically predecease their partners; divorce later in life has become more common; and a great majority of females will face living out their lives without a marriage partner. Many women must work well into their retirement years and fail to have a comfortable and secure life. In the United States, 70 percent of the elderly poor are women, who often live in conditions inferior to what they were accustomed to during their younger years. If you are the average woman over 60 years of age, then your annual income is only $6,300, and that *includes* what you receive from Social Security and pension.

In one national survey, it was discovered that most women have never made investments that would secure their financial freedom, and they do not know what they will receive from pensions or Social Security. Most women have never made a financial plan for retirement. And if they became disabled, they would have no source of income replacement. Most women in their 30s and 40s do not even want to think about retirement because they are too busy or still feel too young and carefree to bother. Suddenly they may discover financial distress at their doorstep because of a job loss, divorce, or medical emergency. A female family practitioner told us that between 60 percent and 80 percent of the women come in for medical care resulting from stress that is usually caused by money problems.

The Plight of a Single Working Mother

The plight of the single working mother in the financial world is one that is overlooked and misunderstood by many. Her financial problems are not necessarily a matter of dysfunctional spending as much as they are the burdens of being caught in the position of extreme responsibility (parenting), along with financial limits on earning potential.

An example of such a situation is Kimberly—an intelligent and beautiful twenty-nine-year-old woman. Kimberly was recently divorced and has a two-year-old child to support. She also has great computer skills, an

Associate's degree from a business school, and a friendly, outgoing personality. If any woman has an outstanding chance to advance to higher levels of income in her chosen field, it is Kimberly. However, the reality is that in a typical administrative assistant or secretarial position, the maximum annual salary is in the $25,000 to $30,000 range. Kimberly is presently making only $29,000 per year.

In our present financial system, the lower-paid women often do most of the work. When it's time for raises or cost-of-living increases based on a percentage of salary, guess what? The lower-paid female gets the smallest salary increase. Kimberly's story reflects that the door is sealed very tightly on this financial trap.

She wanted to buy insurance and invest in her and her baby's future; however, after taxes were deducted from her $29,000 income, she was left with approximately $20,000 dollars per year, or less than $1,800 per month. As we all know, the working woman is expected to dress well to uphold a professional image at the office. With outfits costing $100 and up, and purses and shoes ranging from $35 to $150, this could cause Kimberly to spend much of her hard-earned money primarily on dressing professionally. Let's see how Kimberly spends her money.

Kimberly's child care is very expensive since, as a responsible parent, she wants quality care. Kimberly is spending approximately $300 per month for child care, not to mention her child's clothes, diapers, and miscellaneous supplies. Her rent on a modest two-bedroom apartment is $465 per month, and her utilities are an additional $100.

Of course she needs an automobile since she lives in a town with no public transportation system. So she pays a $350 car note. The insurance, fuel, maintenance, and license tags will cost another $250 per month.

Kimberly now has approximately $335 per month that has not been allotted to these fixed expenses. With this small amount she must buy groceries, pay parking, pay the clothing bill, and take care of miscellaneous repairs and medical bills. She can then take whatever is left over and save for her future!

Obviously, you can see the dilemma that our highly inflated, financially disproportionate society has caused the Kimberlys of America. Many men do not understand this dilemma because they assume that $30,000 a year for the professional woman is a lot of money.

Many working mothers do not get child support on a regular basis either. In Kimberly's case, support from her ex-husband is only enough to pay for the day care expense. But she is under water each month that child support does not show up in the mailbox.

The Ever-Accelerating Treadmill That Leads Nowhere

Many times we get caught on a treadmill where we measure our success and happiness by the size of our last paycheck or last week's sales activity.

For example, Paul was a thirty-one-year-old man when he first sought financial counseling. He was a tall, dark, handsome 220-pound athletic type. He had a tremendous drive to be successful and overcome some old ghosts in his past. His family background was such that he had forever seen financial failure, excessive spending, phone calls promising the "check is in the mail," and penalties for checks that bounced. He felt compelled to financially succeed because of his fear of failure; he wanted to prove he could do it. Part of his life was lived in "survival mode" with fears of not having enough, being subjected to the same humiliation he saw in his parents' home, or being considered a fake. The other part of his life was motivated by anger because of the abuse he had witnessed. His burning desire to succeed was evident, but it was a neurotic drive manifested by anger and a chip on his shoulder.

Paul is now in his 40s. Over the years, his family history has started to reveal how he grew up in a home where the family lived in constant fear of the "repo man" and dodged creditors on a regular basis. They were dishonest to creditors and lived day to day without any surplus savings for those unforeseen expenses or emergencies.

As the years have passed, Paul has begun to learn some valuable lessons about himself and his money. He has learned that he's spent much of his adult life chasing the financial rainbow—the belief system that *more and nicer will make me happy*. Owning a 4,500 square-foot house, a Mercedes, car phone, compact disc player, computer, and big screen TV left him feeling like an indentured servant. He was frequently depressed. He spoke to friends of feeling empty in the process of earning and spending his money. For years his spending managed to increase to his new levels of earning, until he finally felt trapped on a never-ending, stress-testing, ever-accelerating treadmill.

Paul did not have many close friends, although he had attempted to reach out to some people by being the life of the party, giving gifts, and picking up the tab. In retrospect, his ride on the financial treadmill of life started in early childhood as a way to escape family fears and bolster self-esteem. As he ran faster and faster, he could always sense those old fears were not far behind.

Luckily, Paul is beginning to reprioritize his objectives after assessing the misconceptions on which he had centered his adult life: More money, more power, and total immersion of oneself in work would provide the solution for all of life's problems . . . and lead to happiness.

The Less We Want, the Less We Need

One of the toughest problems in our society that relates to dysfunctional spending is that of wants versus needs. Big-screen TVs, Mercedes, large homes, boats, and Rolex watches can be defined as wants. Needs are basic essentials such as food, clothing, shelter, and education, which must be acquired on a day-to-day basis in order to live a normal, productive life.

Many people have confused wants and needs; basic needs are often replaced by wants. One of our wants is basic self-esteem. For example, "I want to feel better about myself, and I want people to look up to me and respect me." "I want to be somebody." This may get expressed in our dysfunctional financial lifestyle as "I want to purchase something to make me feel better."

The conflict between wants and needs is a constant issue in a typical day of financial counseling. An all-too-frequent scenario involves an individual who needs cash to maintain his or her inflated standard of living and wants to borrow money to continue dysfunctional spending habits.

One summer morning, a few years ago, a client named Dave called his insurance agent. Dave was a proud man whose voice was normally deep and confident. But, with anxiety in his voice, he explained the financial troubles burdening his independent oil company. He lived in a 4,000-square-foot house, had a maid, a staff of ten employees, a country club membership, and two luxury cars. He asked how much cash he had in his $750,000 life insurance policy. A few calculations later his agent gave him the amount of $1,200.

You could hear the anxiety mounting in Dave's voice . . . then a pause . . . and suddenly he said, "Let's cancel the policy and get the cash because I'm down to $1,500 in my account, and payroll is coming due." When asked why he would not consider a bank loan first, he replied, "I have already borrowed to the max."

———— • • • ————

Debt is the worst poverty.

Thomas Fuller

———— • • • ————

We often pay our debts not because it is only fair that we should, but to make future loans easier.

Francois de La Rochefoucauld,
French author

———— • • • ————

The High Price of "Toys"

With a combined forty years of working with families who experience stressful, dysfunctional, financial life-styles, we, the authors, see one problem that continues to rear its ugly head over and over again. The problem is the lack of clear communication between husband and wife about how the family money should be managed. The spouses may have different goals which have never been discussed. Often there is not a written plan and how such a plan should be carried out.

One client used to call and say that he could not save money because his wife could not curtail her spending. He would elaborate on her spending sprees and lack of regard for financial security through savings.

Finally, both the husband and the wife came into the office to work on a financial plan. What began to unravel in the conversation was the fact that the husband was constantly charging expensive meals, pouring all his spare money into a boat he did not use, and was consistently writing checks that he would not record, making it difficult for his wife to maintain an accurate checking account balance.

This example amplifies one of the phenomena that persist in many families—the old cliché that "the difference between men and boys is the price of their toys." Men typically spend more money on large expenses, but don't buy as frequently. Women spend less per purchase, but buy more often. We are not sure who wins the Spendthrift of the Year Award. But in total dollars, the award probably goes to the men.

— • • • —

Never ask of money spent
Where the spender thinks it went.
Nobody was ever meant
To remember or invent
What he did with every cent.

Robert Frost

— • • • —

Success Is a Financial Addiction

Bill was a handsome, fun-loving, confident professional baseball player. He spent ten years in the major leagues. Both teams he played for could always count on him to make the crucial plays. He never "choked," and his great arm could peg the plate from the right field fence. All of his teammates respected his leadership, and many idolized his success.

Bill was making a six-figure income and was spending everything he brought home. He was very proud and loved to celebrate with his friends and family after his victories. His friends and relatives were always glad to let him pick up the check. Nothing was too good or too much to symbolize his success. He enjoyed being able to treat his wife like a queen; she was the perfect image of royalty with her beautiful million-dollar clothes.

Bill's success gave him more money than he ever imagined, and he felt money could solve almost any problem. Consequently, he began to overspend. It became impossible for him to gain financial control even though he hired experts to help. He asked them to set up a budget; but when the mood struck him, he would abandon the budget for the pleasures of the moment. He did not want to take responsibility for his spending behavior, but wanted the experts to make decisions for him. They set up an allowance for him, but he would still overspend if he was in the mood. He always found a way to beat the system!

On a cold day in December, a doctor confirmed Bill's worst fears: The knee that had been a chronic source of pain for three seasons would need major reconstructive surgery. All the next spring, Bill exercised with all his motivation to rehabilitate his knee. Eventually, he was able to run, jump, and throw again. The teammates welcomed him back into spring training camp with great excitement and anticipation.

However, in the first week of April the manager gave him some bad news: Bill's position was being filled by a younger player. The pain Bill had felt in his knee did not compare to the pain he felt when he realized his salary had ended and his days of frivolous spending had left him little money for the future.

As reality set in, Bill and his family decided it was time to reevaluate their financial situation and to regroup. The family went through depression, a sense of emptiness, and culture shock. They could no longer afford the expense of expert advisors, nor could they find creative ways not "to pay the piper." They took control of their own checkbook. They devised a budget. They discovered that life could be happy with less and felt a tremendous source of pride now that they were in control of their financial direction. Today, Bill is a very successful business person who feels a sense of control over his own destiny, even on an income less than he once made. Bill and his wife both claim they are much happier today and describe their years at the top as being in a drug-induced state of excess.

——— • • • ———

We are stripped bare by the curse of plenty.
Winston Churchill

——— • • • ———

The Two-Income Family Becomes One

This is a story about the Johnson family, who appeared to be heading in the right financial direction. The husband was a doctor, and the wife had a business degree and had worked to put her husband through medical school. They had two beautiful daughters and a handsome son. Mrs. Johnson now worked to manage Dr. Johnson's office. His practice was starting to grow beyond their wildest dreams, and a fitting reward was the stately home they had built. Although they were still paying for his medical school loans and the loan to open his practice, their house note was easily paid every month. Dr. Johnson wanted to protect his family, so he carried a $1 million life insurance policy.

Life was going along as close to perfect as one could imagine. Then one day Dr. Johnson began to cough up blood. He had not been feeling well for a few months but had been too busy to do anything about it. He finally consulted a fellow physician and discovered he had lung cancer. He had not smoked for six years and at first could not believe the diagnosis. He requested a second opinion which confirmed the first. Treatments and surgery left him weak and unable to work very much. In a whole year he was only able to see patients forty-eight days. Therefore, his income dropped dramatically. They closed his office, and his wife went to work in another physician's office.

It appears that Dr. Johnson is going to beat the cancer, but he and his wife just filed for bankruptcy. Although he was insured against death, he was not insured against disability.

Are You Really Enjoying the Ride, or Just Holding On?

This book is for all of us. We have all sought a dream and worked hard to make it come true. We have studied for the right education and developed our talents. We have tried to make ends meet. And we have also tried to have the right jeans, perfume, shampoo, microwave, VCR, car, and house. We have collected the stuff the advertisers try to convince us will make us happier, more attractive, and more fulfilled.

Now we can shop in the comfort of our own living rooms as we watch television shows that feed our insatiable quest for more things. But are our lives better when we have more stuff or just more full of things that break, commitments to meet, and responsibilities without significant meaning or value? For that matter, do we even know *what* we truly value?

——— • • • ———

Life is not having and getting, but being and becoming.

——— • • • ———

The Ingredients of Financial Wellness

This first section of this book has been an introduction to financial dysfunction versus financial wellness. In Section II you will be given the opportunity to assess your personal financial life and decide which areas you need to manage more effectively. In Section III you will learn basic knowledge for financial wellness. In Section IV you will be exposed to guidelines for changing your financial lifestyle. Savor each guideline slowly, as if you're learning to differentiate fine spices. Only after you can recognize the spices of life you want to use for your own special recipe can you become the master chef of your life.

The TOTAL PERSON Program for Financial Lifestyle Changes

The TOTAL PERSON Program
for Financial Lifestyle Changes

T *IME*

O *UT*

T *O*

A *SSESS AND* **A** *LTER*

L *IFESTYLE*

P *LANNING / BUDGET*

E *MOTIONAL SPENDING*

R *ETIREMENT*

S *AVINGS AND SPENDING CONTROL*

O *PTIONS AND OPPORTUNITIES*

N *EEDS AND NECESSITIES*

CHAPTER SIX

Financial Management for the TOTAL PERSON

A bishop then must be blameless, the husband of one wife, temperate, sober-minded, of good behavior, hospitable, able to teach; not given to wine, not violent, not greedy for money, but gentle, not quarrelsome, not covetous.

1 Timothy 3:2-3

— • • • —

Time Out To Assess Lifestyle

If we have dysfunctional financial lifestyles, we can expect our bodies, minds, spirits, and relationships to be affected. Let's take an honest look at how we are responding to our modern fiscal lifestyles. Let's also examine our strengths and weaknesses in terms of good habits, as well as poorly developed life skills. This is what Section II of this book is all about.

If you have a child who is sick, you may take him or her to the family doctor. The family doctor is usually a general practitioner who will determine the proper diagnosis and treatment. Tests may confirm it is a problem of the bones, and the doctor may send you to an orthopedic specialist. If it is a problem of the heart or circulation, then he or she may send you to a cardiologist. First, an assessment of the type of problem you have will determine the appropriate intervention or what type of specialist you need.

Section II is like having your blood analyzed or an X-ray taken. You will discover what areas of your financial lifestyle need the most healing. You will be able to calculate a Financial Quotient to help you understand the areas of your fiscal lifestyle that are dysfunctional, as well as the changes you can make to help ensure a long, happy, healthy life.

———— • • • ————

Man spends the first half of his life acquiring habits that shorten the second half of his life.

———— • • • ————

Discover What Your PERSON Is Like

Take the time to assess all the areas of your TOTAL PERSON: Planning/Budget; Emotional Spending; Retirement; Savings and Spending Control (Credit Cards and Deficit Spending); Options and Opportunities; and Needs and Necessities. Assess how you respond to your financial world. You may have strengths in one or more areas, and be dangerously out of control in others.

Current Financial Lifestyle

Our financial lifestyle and fiscal survival techniques have a major impact on how well we manage our total life, how happy we are, how productive we are, and how fully actualized and maximized our potential is becoming. Many people take better care of their cars than they do their own credit ratings. Some people may have low self-esteem, bottle up their feelings, or have difficulty giving and receiving affection, so they use purchasing as a way to feel better. Some pursue more and more material possessions, only to still feel empty and lonely inside. Sometimes, as we become responsible adults, we forget how to play and have fun; but we take expensive vacations only to sit on the beach and think about work. Sometimes we get confused about our real values and the purpose of our lives. We may isolate ourselves from close friendships and family. Sometimes the balance between work, family, and personal time gets terribly out of control. We live in a society where our occupation may become our identity, and we forget who we really are.

Complete the scales on the following pages to assess your financial lifestyle and discover your Financial Quotient. Be honest as you try to discover the areas of your financial lifestyle that may be out of balance. Remember, you are not competing with anyone, just discovering yourself.

———•·•———

Before you can break out of prison, you must first realize you're locked up.

———•·•———

Financial Management for the TOTAL PERSON

Planning and Budgets

Perhaps the most important part of our financial lifestyle is the care we take with planning, budgeting, and using our available resources. If we do not plan our fiscal lifestyle, then we may find all the other areas of our life harder to manage.

The budget is the foundation of the planning process. Without a budget there is no game plan for the future, and there are no results from the past to review.

Budgeting takes discipline and requires us to make a list of all current debts—such items as food, clothing, car repairs, home maintenance, and quarterly and annual insurance premiums. Many people make the mistake of not taking into account the nonfixed monthly expenses, such as vacation, Christmas, birthdays, income tax, emergency funds, medical bills.

Can you imagine sailing out to sea without a compass or a chart? A budget is much like a compass that gives you a true reading of the direction you are going or want to go. Without it "we know not where we have been or where we are going."

Emergency Funds and Budgeting

When doing the budgeting process, one should always allow for those surprise miscellaneous expenses—for example, a family illness or unexpected plumbing repair. An emergency fund equal to ninety days living expenses is necessary to cover such expenses.

Another secret to making the budget process work is to take all annual and quarterly bills and divide them into equal monthly payments to determine what to allow monthly for the future payments of a debt. The future bill should be planned for as if it is due month to month. A good example is the homeowner who pays his own property taxes once a year. If he does not budget for it, then he receives a huge bill right at Christmas time.

We also do plastic surgery to our wallets to help the budget process. This simply means cutting up all credit cards except for one major credit card and one gasoline card. Multiple cards are only a temptation to fall into the trap of credit purchases with installment payments.

Complete the following questionnaire to assess how well you do at planning and budgeting.

PART 1: Planning and Budgeting

Yes/No (1 point per "yes" answer)

_____ 1. Do you have a written budget?

_____ 2. Do you have a written, organized cash flow statement?

_____ 3. Do you have an emergency fund equal to ninety days budget needs?

_____ 4. Do you have a Christmas, birthday, holiday, vacation, and miscellaneous family activity fund?

_____ 5. Do you charge on one major credit card only?

_____ 6. Do you have a monthly food allowance?

_____ 7. Do you have a monthly clothing allowance?

_____ 8. Do you regularly allow for savings?

_____ 9. Do you escrow or save money for annual fees, licenses, and taxes?

_____ 10. Do you avoid the use of automatic teller machines?

_____ TOTAL "YES" SCORES FOR PLANNING

Emotional Spending

Our self-esteem develops from the moment of our birth. We learn we are worthwhile, even with all our limitations or faults. Or we learn we "should have done better" or "have to be perfect." We learn to evaluate ourselves by our own values or by the expectations of others.

We learn to openly communicate our wants, needs, thoughts, and feelings. Or we learn to keep it all bottled up. We sometimes do not learn how to say no without feeling guilty. And sometimes we may have difficulty giving and receiving affection.

———•••———

We attract what we feel worthy of.

———•••———

Emotional Spending, or When Too Much Is Not Enough

Emotional spending is very much overlooked as a problem in our country. With all the high-priced advertising thrown at us, along with plastic cards with higher credit limits than ever before, the Spendaholic is in real trouble. Unfortunately, all the spending and all the charging often is incapable of filling the needs in our souls, quieting the pain in our hearts, or satisfying our need for fellowship and emotional closeness. In all these cases, no matter how much we buy, it is not enough. "Too much just ain't enough."

In our country, most spending is emotional. There can be healthy, unemotional spending. There can also be healthy, emotional spending. But too much of our spending may be unhealthy emotional spending. Unhealthy emotional spending is when we are trying to spend enough money and purchase enough stuff to make us feel better about ourselves, to raise our self-esteem. This type of spending typically leads us into the trap of having to have the nicest of everything, with every purchase.

Will the Seiko or Timex watch work, or does it need to be a diamond-studded "Presidential" Rolex watch? Does the nice Buick or Chevrolet get the job done, or is the Mercedes sedan with chrome wheels necessary? Does the

$65 pair of dress shoes suffice, or do we need the $200 Italian loafers?

Another form of unhealthy emotional spending is the addiction of credit card purchasing out of boredom, depression, or anxiety. There is nothing like going to a mall on a cold rainy day and walking around looking for specials that will make us feel better. The problem is that many times, after we get home with these purchases we didn't need, we feel guilty about buying them. And once again "too much just ain't enough."

Now for the good news: healthy emotional spending. If we know we need a new car, or a more dependable car, and we fall in love with the dolled-up version on the showroom floor, it's OK to buy it as long as our budget can afford it. Often we will spend more on a loved one than we would on ourselves, but if our budget can afford it, then the purchase is simply an expression of our love. The words *emotional spending* do not have to be negative as long as the emotion is one of good judgment.

Complete the following questionnaire to help assess how affected you are by emotional spending.

PART 2: Emotional Spending

Yes/No

_____ 1. Do you go shopping when you are lonely, angry, depressed, or bored?
_____ 2. Do you frequently experience guilt about spending too much money?
_____ 3. Do you feel you deserve the best and therefore pay more on certain items than you can really afford?
_____ 4. Do you purchase items because they are a "good buy," even though you do not need them?
_____ 5. Do you pick up the tab so people will like you?

_____ 6. Do you possess "monuments to the ego," such as fancy cars, jewelry, homes, and furs, that cause stress to your budget?

_____ 7. Do you judge your success in terms of numbers (for example, bigger house, more money, etc.)?

_____ 8. Do you judge others by their income or possessions?

_____ 9. Do you feel the following bumper sticker message applies to you? "I owe, I owe, so it's off to work I go."

_____ 10. Do you frequently feel the need to buy things for relatives or friends to prove that you love them?

_____ TOTAL "NO" SCORES FOR EMOTIONAL SPENDING

Retirement Planning

What does retirement mean to you? For most of us it means to reach age sixty-five and live on a modest income for the rest of our lives. However, that's not the way retirement really works. In today's society, retirement can come at age 45, 55, 60, and so on. To retire means we will have the ability to maintain a comfortable lifestyle without actively working. This can take place at any age if the planning process has taken place.

The key ingredient to retirement is planning ahead. Most Americans have not done well in this area because of procrastination. We always feel that we can start the process of planning for retirement tomorrow; if we do not, the Social Security system will take care of us. Over 80 percent of the retired people surveyed in our country live on Social Security as their main means of financial support.

In planning for retirement, an investment strategy needs to be developed according to different age groups.

An age group of people under thirty should put approximately 75 percent of all their savings into growth type investments, such as common stocks or bonds, and 25 percent of their savings into conservative investments, such as government securities, CDs at banks, or annuities with insurance companies.

For those people who are now thirty to forty-five years of age, the investment strategy mix should be to place approximately 60 percent of savings assets into growth and 40 percent into more conservative investments. At forty-six to fifty-five years of age the strategy should move more to a 50/50 mix.

Finally, when approaching the fifty-six to sixty-five retirement age, the mix of growth investments and conservative investments should reverse. During this period, 35 to 40 percent of the savings dollars should be placed into growth (more risky) type of investments, and 60 to 65 percent should be invested in the more conservative side.

The breakdown we have just covered minimizes your risks when you need the money for retirement but allows you to be a little riskier when you are younger and trying to plant as many seeds for growth as possible. This means that while you are young and planning for retirement, the majority of the investment dollars should be put into the growth side in order for you to enjoy the fruits of labor in later life. Hopefully, when you are ready for retirement, you will have a wagon full of the fruits you harvested from all the planting you did in your younger years.

In planning retirement we should also take advantage of two areas of tax credits. The first is an Individual Retirement Account (IRA), which will allow a person without a company retirement plan to deposit $2,000 annually into an approved investment account of their choice and take a tax deduction.

The other plan often available to employees is a 401K plan. If presented the opportunity, the employee who is interested in retirement should definitely take advantage of this plan. This plan will allow your employer to match your payroll deposit. Your entire deposit is tax deductible, and all its earnings are tax deferred.

Retirement does not just happen to us. It is a privilege that must be seriously planned if you really hope to accomplish it. Complete the following questionnaire to assess how well you are doing at planning for retirement.

PART 3: Retirement Planning

Yes/No

_____ 1. Do you have an Individual Retirement Account (IRA)?

_____ 2. Do you have a company-sponsored retirement account or 401K account?

_____ 3. Do you feel that retirement planning is for the young?

_____ 4. Do you feel that retirement age can be less than sixty-five if you plan properly?

_____ 5. Do you feel that Social Security will not be ample for your retirement needs?

_____ 6. Do you have sources of passive income, such as rental properties, planned for your retirement?

_____ 7. Do you have short-term investments, such as mutual funds, that will provide you income during your retirement?

_____ 8. Do you have long-term investments, such as tax-deferred annuities, that will provide you tax-deferred income during your retirement?

_____ 9. Do you have a current financial statement to keep track of your retirement planning results?

___ 10. Do you have a Will to protect the disposition of your retirement assets?

___ TOTAL "YES" SCORES FOR RETIREMENT

Savings and Spending Control

What is savings and spending control? Most Americans are not saving and are out of spending control. A recommended savings concept for most households is a minimum of 5 percent of take-home pay. Ten percent would be even better. As we discussed earlier in this chapter, a budget is necessary to deal with savings and spending control.

Many people we have talked with feel that saving money is something you do if you have spent all the money you want; if, by chance, there is anything left, you attempt to save.

Saving must become a planned activity called "pay yourself first." We spend our lives paying our creditors our mortgages, car payments, and credit cards and forget about paying ourselves. It's OK to live for today, but the "to-heck-with-tomorrow" theory does not get the job done. Tomorrow does come eventually, and there is always a day of reckoning when it comes to money.

In the area of spending control it is important to practice the word *control*. Many people allow their spending to control them, instead of their controlling spending. As discussed in the Emotional Spending section, many of us are controlled by the urge to spend money in order to deal with our low self-esteem. By contrast, spending control means using good judgment. It is important to make sure discipline is used to allow for basic monthly expenses while being able to draw the line between wants and needs.

Complete the following questionnaire to help assess how well you do at controlling your spending habits and saving money.

PART 4: Savings and Spending Control

Yes/No

_____ 1. Do you save at least 5 percent of your take-home pay?

_____ 2. Does your savings stay in a special interest-bearing account?

_____ 3. Do you own stock, bonds, mutual funds, or real estate investments?

_____ 4. Do you pay off the balances of credit cards monthly rather than incur high interest-rate charges?

_____ 5. Do you have at least 50 percent of your savings in high-yield growth investments such as mutual funds?

_____ 6. Do you have ninety days of monthly budgeted expenses in savings?

_____ 7. Do you allow for unexpected expenses?

_____ 8. Do you have some form of automatic savings withdrawn from your paycheck?

_____ 9. If you have children, have you started savings accounts with them to teach them the value of savings?

_____ 10. Do you have an education/self-improvement fund started for yourself, spouse, and children?

_____ TOTAL "YES" SCORES FOR SAVINGS AND SPENDING CONTROL

Options and Opportunities

We all have options about how financially healthy we are going to be. Regardless of monthly income, we have the responsibility and option to save, invest, and plan for the future.

Many of us find excuses to justify financial dysfunction and lack of planning. In talking to clients, one thing that is constantly prevalent is that often the people who make the least amount of annual income do the best job of saving and getting the most mileage out of the savings dollar.

Though people choose their occupations for the future, many blame financial devastation on their employment. But they have options and choices. For example, if our problem is that our occupation is holding us back, then we should change jobs. Unfortunately, many of us get caught up in a cycle of job security, even if we are miserable. We must remember that "job security is in us, not the job." Our country affords us many options and opportunities, and it's up to us to take advantage of them. It is very easy for us to constantly blame someone else for our financial woes.

Financial opportunities come a person's way approximately seven times in a lifetime. This means that most of us will have some exceptional financial opportunity cross our path seven times in our lifelong journey. The question is, will we be prepared to take advantage of these opportunities? Most people are not because they have no cash resources. There are no cash resources because of poor planning, no savings, and poor spending control.

When financial opportunity comes our way, we must be prepared to act and not react. React is when we say, "Gee, I wish I had the money to do that." Act is when we put procrastination, fear, and doubts aside and take prudent financial action. We must always remember that it is our option to seize the financial opportunities of life. Complete the following questionnaire to assess how well you do at taking advantage of your financial opportunities.

———•••———

While I am busy with little things, I am not required to do greater things.

St. Francis de Sales

———•••———

PART 5: Options and Opportunities

Yes/No

_____ 1. Do you feel you have the opportunity to do better financially?

_____ 2. Do you feel you have control over your employment and income?

_____ 3. If a good financial opportunity presents itself, do you have the resources to take advantage of it?

_____ 4. Do you feel that you have the financial knowledge to make proper financial decisions?

_____ 5. Do you feel that you are in control of your personal security?

_____ 6. Do you feel you receive fair compensation for the work you perform?

_____ 7. Do you live within your means?

_____ 8. Do you believe that financial opportunities will present themselves throughout your life if you are prepared?

_____ 9. Do you take total responsibility for your financial wellness?

_____ 10. Do you believe we live in a do-it-yourself world?

_____ TOTAL "YES" SCORES FOR OPTIONS AND OPPORTUNITIES

Needs And Necessities

"I need everything I want." How many of us are guilty of this statement? In our world of glitter, plastic, and ego, it is easy to confuse needs and wants. Let's look at a list of *needs:* food, clothing, shelter, education, retirement planning, transportation, emergency funds, and medical insurance.

We certainly can justify much of our spending in these areas of needs. When addressing needs, it is easy to go beyond our definitions of true needs into what we just want. For example, should everyone have a 6,000 square-foot home with a pool and a red Porsche for transportation? This is not to say that there is anything wrong with owning these, but they go beyond the basic needs we have listed.

In working with people for years, we have discovered that most people will focus their money mainly on food, clothing, shelter, and transportation. These same people may devote only a small portion of their resources, if any, to retirement planning, education, emergency funds, and insurance.

Let's look at a typical list of *wants* in our everyday life: large home, expensive car, big-screen TV, exotic vacation, video camera, jewelry, boat, and second home. The authors enjoy some of these wants at this stage of their lives. But there was a time when investments or education took precedence over fulfilling these wants. It is important for us to put our needs and wants into proper perspective.

Many times what we feel is a need is really a want. Some of us feel the need to always own the best of everything or the need to always pick up the tab at a restaurant. These types of needs fall into the personal acceptance category and the need to feel better about ourselves. These needs can never truly be satisfied by spending money, since they really relate to a deep-down-inside feeling of low self-esteem. By completing the questionnaire, we need to ask ourselves: "Do I really need what I want?"

———•••———

The highest reward for a person's toil is not what they get for it, but what they become by it.

———•••———

PART 6: Needs And Necessities

Yes/No

_____ 1. Do you feel that food, clothing, shelter, and education are needs?

_____ 2. Do you usually get what you need before you get what you want?

_____ 3. Do you feel you do not need a big-screen TV, Rolex watch, big home, etc., to be happy?

_____ 4. Do you feel needs satisfy survival instincts?

_____ 5. Do you feel that you have control of your needs vs. wants?

_____ 6. Do you feel medical insurance is a necessity?

_____ 7. Do you feel that life insurance is important in your estate planning?

_____ 8. Do you feel that material possessions have little to do with helping you feel spiritually at peace?

_____ 9. Do you feel that your desire for wants is in balance with your resources?

_____ 10. Have you stopped trying to "keep up with the Joneses" in order to be happy?

_____ TOTAL "YES" SCORES FOR NEEDS AND NECESSITIES

What Your Financial Lifestyle Scores Mean

If you scored less than 8 points for any one scale, then you need to examine that area of your financial life to decide if you need to make changes. If you scored 5 to 7, your level of financial wellness is about average but needs to be improved. If you scored 4 or below, that area of your financial life may be dangerously out of control. The chapters of Sections III and IV of this book will give you specific suggestions about how to enhance the individual areas of your financial lifestyle. Go back and look at the individual items in each scale to understand specifically what changes may be important for you.

When you go back and review your scores then record below your total for each scale.

_____ 1. Planning (page 61)
_____ 2. Emotional Spending (page 64)
_____ 3. Retirement (page 67)
_____ 4. Spending & Savings (page 68)
_____ 5. Opportunities & Options (page 70)
_____ 6. Needs & Necessities (page 72)

_____ Total for All Six Financial Lifestyle Scales equals your *Financial Quotient*

What Your **Financial Quotient** *Means*

When you complete all six financial lifestyle scales, then add all six scores together to obtain your Financial Quotient (FQ). If your FQ was 45 to 60, then some areas of your financial lifestyle may be dysfunctional and need improvement, but you are doing many of the things that will be important to experience financial wellness. If your FQ was 30 to 44, you have some of the attitudes and actions that may lead you to financial wellness, but you need to seriously look at the areas that caused you to score lower. If you scored below 30, you run the risk of increased stress because of financial dysfunction. Multiple areas of your financial life may be dangerously out of control, and a secure retirement may be in jeopardy.

Pay particular attention to those individual scale scores that were less than 4. Knowledge of the scales that contributed to lowering your FQ will help you decide which areas of financial management need the most work. In the next section of this book you will begin learning how to alter your financial lifestyle. You may also benefit from discussing your financial lifestyle with a professional or beginning a self-improvement program directed toward the specific areas where you scored lowest. Even if most of your scale scores were not in the significant ranges, you may want to examine whether any scales were "valleys," or low points, in comparison with other scales. This may suggest the areas of your lifestyle that could benefit from additional enhancement.

SECTION III

Basic Knowledge and Steps for Financial Wellness

CHAPTER SEVEN

What We Don't Know about Financial Institutions Can Cost Us!

Then Jesus went into the temple of God and drove out all those who bought and sold in the temple, and overturned the tables of the moneychangers and the seats of those who sold doves. And He said to them, "It is written, 'My house shall be called a house of prayer,' but you have made it a 'den of thieves.'"

Matthew 21:12-13

• • •

All financial institutions are selling something to us at all times. Most people want to make sure they don't make a mistake financially and trust the wrong person with their money. The interesting phenomenon, however, is that the people who want to be the most cautious often end up making the worst choices about products and their selection of advisors. Typically, it is easy for all of us to make bad decisions because we live in a financial world that has us set up to help others succeed at our own expense.

———•••———

A financier is a pawn-broker with imagination.
Arthur Wing Pinero,
English dramatist

———•••———

Loss of the Family Farm

A story we recently heard seemed to reflect the cold, hard reality that financial institutions are not your friends, but simply another business. A farmer who was also a reserve naval captain returned from less than four months of fighting for our country in the Persian Gulf War. He had never been away from his family that long and had for the first time missed spending Christmas with his wife and three daughters. He stepped off the plane when he arrived back home. He scanned the yellow-ribboned crowds of people as he looked for his wife, but she was nowhere to be found. Hastily making a call home, he discovered from a family friend that his wife had been admitted to a psychiatric hospital. She had a "nervous breakdown" after the family's farm equipment was sold at a bank auction.

Even though this farmer was not behind on any debts when he went to serve his country, the bank had sold equipment that had been appraised for nearly a quarter of a million dollars for only $80,000. The equipment that would have paid off all the farm debts, paid the house note, and given the family money to live was gone. The bank had sold it in a way that would bring the least amount of money—auction. The bank had sold the equipment, even though this man was honorably serving our country and was gone for less than four months. The bank had sold it, even though it violated a law that was meant to protect our servicemen from such atrocities.

This family was devastated. The husband has been trying to find a job and clips food coupons while waiting. The wife got out of the psychiatric hospital and found a job as an administrative assistant. She also developed a neck problem, but the company she works for changed health insurance policies. Now her medical problem is not covered because it is a "pre-existing condition." Their children work to pay their own college tuition. The family makes about 20 percent of what their income was when they had the farm. They finally had to file bankruptcy, but they are still too proud to collect food stamps.

A story such as this should never occur in our great country, but it happens every day. Over 90 percent of all Americans fail financially, and part of the reason is that so many people make a living off of our money. You are the only person who has your best financial interests at heart. Therefore, it is your responsibility to learn how other people make a living off of your money. Your banker or stockbroker can become a friend, but their job is to make their family a living. Let us give you some examples of how people make a living off of your money.

Why Your Banker Wants to Be Your Friend

Your friendly banker may suggest you play it safe and put all of your money into certificates of deposits (CDs) for a year at 2 to 5 percent interest. He does not tell you that he gets a bonus annually or quarterly based upon the number of CDs he has brought into the bank during that period. He does not usually explain to you that by the time you pay 28 percent income tax out of the 2 to 5 percent interest that you will have 1 to 3 percent left. He also does not usually explain about inflation, which has averaged 3 percent per year over the last five years. This may leave you with a net loss or only earning 1 percent on your "safe investment." One reason you may not be completely informed about what is in your best financial interest is your banker's own conflict of interest; his bonus will be less if he fails to sell enough CDs, and his or her job may even be in jeopardy.

Let's continue to look at banks and some examples of other little-known methods they use to ensure *their* success at *your* expense. Why do banks try to sell us credit life insurance and/or disability insurance when we make a well-collateralized loan? It is not to protect your family's financial future. The main reason that these programs are a major money maker for the institution, is because the bank and the banker get a *commission*.

This is the way it works: The banker has a special life insurance license for selling credit life. For every policy the banker gets you to buy, both the bank and the banker may get a commission from the insurance company. The commission may be paid to the banker in the form of a bonus. If a banker does not meet certain goals or quotas for insurance sales, his or her job may be at risk. This is just one other little piece of your pie that is eaten by someone else.

Have you ever wondered why some banks and savings and loans now sell annuities to their customers? Again, the main reason is *commission*. Many institutions started realizing that over the past few years they were losing CD money to brokerage houses and insurance companies because annuities have, for the past sixty-five years, paid a higher rate of return than CDs. So, the banks decided to get into the annuity business.

There is a small problem. Anyone selling an annuity must have an insurance license. It would be too difficult to get all bankers licensed, and too expensive to continue the educational requirements. Therefore, the banking institutions decided they could license only one person in the bank, by sending this person to a one- or two-day crash course on insurance. This would allow the bank to sell you annuities through its central person formally signing the necessary documents. Isn't that interesting? But wait! That is not the most important part of the story. The insurance companies that handle the annuities for the banks and savings and loans often have some of the highest charges and withdrawal penalties.

Here's an example: Jane Sorenson was a sixty-two-year-old client who took her CD to renew at the local bank. Her banker talked her into rolling it over into an annuity. What he did *not* tell her was that if she wanted out of the annuity before ten years, she would pay as much as a 15 percent penalty of the original investment amount. What she *was* told was that she would earn an additional 1 percent higher than a CD. That is all she knows. Now, what is wrong with this scenario? First, a good annuity will not have penalties beyond seven years, and the penalties will not exceed 7 percent, in the worst case. Second, the banker may not be knowledgeable due to a non-insurance background. Therefore, he or she may not know how to explain the problem or even know what qualities a good annuity possesses. Third, the bank has chosen the insurance company to do business with which will benefit the banking institution the most. You guessed it! They choose insurance companies which pay the highest commissions. Most good annuities only pay approximately 3 to 3½ percent commission, while poor annuities pay as high as 15 percent commission.

What does all this mean? It means you should probably not buy annuities through banking institutions because of the extra middleman—the bank—which is not necessary.

Now let's continue reviewing how banks may have a conflict of interest when giving us financial advice. Many people in America go into banks and savings and loans to purchase their retirement plans—such as IRAs, KEOGH plans, and SEP (Self-employed retirement) plans—and some companies allow them to manage their 401K plans. Well, guess what? They take the investment dollar to the New Accounts desk, to an employee who does not always understand the penalties, problems, and drawbacks to retirement plans. This employee gladly takes your money and puts it into one of the CDs or annuities that we have been discussing. Your retirement dollars usually go into a low-interest CD. Roughly 70 to 80 percent of the earning in a CD will be eroded by inflation and taxation. You are probably asking yourself, Why do most people do this? Don't they want a "safe investment" from a person who is not a salesman; someone they can trust?

Let's address the word *safe* for a moment: In one respect, *safe* probably is a bank. Every dollar up to $100,000 that we have in a bank is insured. If there was a run on the FDIC insurance tomorrow across the country, the federal deficit would skyrocket; because for every dollar in a CD or savings account, the FDIC only has one to two cents in insurance reserves.

Banks should be used as holding tanks for money such as checking accounts, mad-money accounts, and short-term savings. They should not be used as investment institutions. We will talk more about how to use investment institutions later in this book, but let's look at insurance companies and how they may also have their own best interests at heart, not ours.

— • • • —

The money-changers have fled from their high seats in the temple of our civilization. We may now restore that temple to the ancient truths.
Franklin Delano Roosevelt

— • • • —

Dealing with Insurance Companies

Many times it is difficult for the consumer to know which financial direction to take. Often, even if our desire to plan is strong, it still becomes purely a guess as to which direction to follow, thanks to all the confusing information. One of the most misunderstood areas in the financial world is that of life insurance. The biggest problem with understanding life insurance choices is the fact that the insurance companies offer a cafeteria full of choices and have placed the distribution of these choices in the hands of a commissioned sales force. This, in itself, is not necessarily bad. However, it *can* be.

The major insurance companies in this country have placed both the consumer and the salesperson in a very interesting dilemma. Many of the higher-yielding, im-proved-benefit policies that are the most advantageous for the consumer to purchase also pay the lower commission schedules. In addition, the investment products sold by insurance companies which pay higher yields (such as annuities and mutual funds) pay the smallest commission scale. Obviously, a conflict is created when the best product for the customer over the long term may not be the best product to sell from the salesperson's perspective, due to the higher commission schedule on inferior policies. This is unfortunate, not only for the consumer, but for the sales force, because they are constantly faced with a moral decision on each policy sold. This creates obvious pressure and leaves the consumer doubtful.

The failure rate of salespeople in the insurance business is very high. This means that many insurance people are struggling financially, which adds to the potential problem. There are quality insurance people, but the purchaser should become aware and educated about the choices available.

As if this isn't a complicated enough situation, there is another faction that can influence the quality of the policies and related rates of return and premiums. In the life insurance industry there are two types of life insurance companies—mutual companies and stock insurance companies. Now, what does all this mean? It's very simple, and here's how they differ.

Mutual insurance companies are owned and controlled by the policyholders. There are no stockholders to satisfy and pay dividends distributions. Mutual companies tend to pay smaller commissions to their sales force. And due to the fact that there are no stockholders, many of their policies pay a dividend return to the policyholder annually.

Stock insurance companies are owned by stockholders instead of policyholders. This is an important point, because most of their policies do not pay annual dividends back to the policyholder due to the need to satisfy the stockholders. Some of the stock insurance companies pay higher commissions to the sales force than mutual insurance companies do.

Many times if the policy is not readily identified as a stock or mutual policy, it can be identified in this way: Look for the words *participating* or *nonparticipating*, usually found on the cover of the policy. *Participating* will tell you that the policy pays an annual dividend, which in most cases will identify the company as a mutual insurance company. *Nonparticipating* will tell you that no dividend is paid and that, most likely, this is a stock insurance company policy.

The last potential problem for the consumer of life insurance policies is the compensation "layer" system. This layer basically takes your premium for the first three years and pays for the cost of issuing the policy. The reason it takes so long to cover front-end costs is that there are various layers of commission income for the sales and management staff.

Typically, the home-office vice president will receive an incentive bonus for total sales. The regional sales manager receives an incentive bonus. The local manager and an assistant manager may also receive an incentive bonus. Last but not least, the direct salesperson gets his or her commission. This system creates a tremendous amount of pressure on everyone to sell-sell-sell in order to beat last year's corporate sales volume.

• • •

Insurance is an ingenious modern game of chance in which the player is permitted to enjoy the comfortable conviction that he is beating the man who keeps the table.

Ambrose Bierce

• • •

Buy an annuity cheap, and make your life interesting to yourself and everybody else that watches the speculation.

Charles Dickens

• • •

Dealing with Stock Brokerage and Investment Houses

Obviously, our country is made of many fine investment firms and stockbrokerages. However, not all of their recommendations are in the best interest of the consumer. In most cases, stockbroker compensation is paid at the time of sale, on the front end and the back end. Let us explain: When a stock recommendation is made and a stock purchase takes place, there is a commission paid to the stockbroker. When the stock you have previously purchased is now ready to be sold by you, the broker gets a commission off the value of the present sale of your stock. Therefore, there has been a commission *twice* on the same stock. This is not necessarily bad, but it leaves a lot of room for scrutinizing by the consumer.

Many stockbrokers will be pushed by their firms to recommend stocks that may or may not be the best choices of investment for the investor. Due to the fact that the stockbroker is, for the most part, a commission-driven person, one must be careful of a term called *churning*.

Churning is when a broker continually takes the investor's money and moves it in and out of stocks, usually over a short period of time. This is done to generate commission for the broker time and time again on the same block of money originally invested.

We recommend that most investors, unless very knowledgeable, should stay with mutual funds instead of individual stocks for safer diversification of investment money. This would eliminate the dilemma of churning because mutual funds should be held for three to five years minimum, depending on the type of mutual fund you invest with.

Stocks and stock mutual funds both have inherent risks. They are subject to fluctuations of value based on a variety of factors which even professional stockbrokers cannot always predict. Their value can decrease in contrast to CDs, which have guaranteed principal. However, mutual funds are less prone to fluctuations than individual stocks and should have much higher yields than CDs. Mutual funds only pay a commission one time to the salesperson, and they should not be constantly sold for a short period of time.

When dealing with a stockbroker, you should have him explain to you up front what his strategy for your investments will be, and why he or she has selected that strategy. You should make it clear that you do not want to be changing ships and directions all the time and jumping at hot investment tips which make you have to outguess the stock market.

The irony of the investment business is that for the consumer or investor the best decision is to get investments and hold them through the market trends over a long period of time. For the broker the best situation is to constantly move the investor's money into something new. Could this set us up for potential failure? Whose retirement are you planning for? Yours or the stockbroker's, banker's, or life insurance sales agent's?

Financial sense is knowing that certain men will promise to do certain things, and fail.

Ed Howe

High finance isn't burglary or obtaining money by false pretenses, but rather a judicious selection from the best features of those fine arts.

Finley Peter Dunne,
American journalist

CHAPTER EIGHT

What to Do When You Need Major "Plastic Surgery"

How Do Americans Get into So Much Credit Card Trouble?

Let's look a moment at how Americans get into credit card trouble. First of all, it is very easy to obtain credit cards today; institutions are pushing the cards at every turn. Most Americans are spending 10 to 20 percent more than they make each year. Therefore, credit cards become the obvious haven for $pendaholics.

Overspending usually occurs when an individual has two or more major credit cards with limits of $1,000 to $5,000 per card. As you know, when you charge on revolving credit, you only have to pay a minimum of $20 to $50 per month. Therefore, you can charge from $3,000 to $15,000 with a maximum payment of $60 to $150 per month. However, there is a problem. How is a person that did not have the money to pay $3,000 to $15,000 of debt to begin with, going to pay off their newfound debt *plus* the 21 percent interest charged annually? Within three to four years, the borrowed amount of money will double!

Well, this is easy enough. Just apply for another card with a $5,000 to $10,000 limit, to pay off the first credit card . . . or make a consolidation loan at a bank, to pay off all the credit card debt. The problem with borrowing from the bank is that no one will loan money to a person who's in debt, especially without collateral to secure the loan. *Collateral* are financial possessions or liquid assets that are usually owned only by people who do not really need loans. But wait a minute. What do you think happens to a person who is fortunate enough to get a loan and pay off all the credit cards? Within a year of the transaction, they are usually charging on their cards again plus paying debt services on their newfound bank loan.

Credit Card Addictions: It's Family Tradition

It is estimated that over 200,000 people in Houston, Texas, alone are in debt up to their ears because of credit card addiction. The average debtor seeking help from the Consumer Credit Counseling Service in Houston is thirty-five years old, married with two children, makes about $25,000 a year, and owes $18,000 to twelve different credit card companies. At the extreme is one man who owed $300,000 before taking into consideration his house mortgage and automobile loan!

— • • • —

The way to stop financial joy-riding is to arrest the chauffeur, not the automobile.

Woodrow Wilson

— • • • —

The decadent decade of the 1980s has left a legacy of debt for people everywhere. Our decade-long shopping spree seems to have ended in 1989, but the effects will be felt for years to come. As a nation, we ran up $717 billion in consumer debt. The Consumer Credit Counseling Service in Houston expects to see 42,000 people in just one year. They are probably only reaching 10 to 20 percent of the people who need help, but they have grown in ten years from one office and three staff members to eleven offices and sixty-three staff members.

——— • • • ———

A man in debt is so far a slave.
Ralph Waldo Emerson

——— • • • ———

You Are Never Too Young to Get Started

Rodney N. was only fifteen years old when he got his first credit card "preapproved" application. With no job and no income, except his weekly allowance and extra money for good school performance, he suddenly discovered he was eligible for a "Gold card" from a major credit card company. Like any youngster would be, he was ecstatic about his new purchasing power. Fortunately for him, his mother destroyed the elegantly presented package.

The Major Causes of Credit Card Overextension

There are several reasons why people may find themselves being buried under the weight of credit card payments. Perhaps the most common is simply mismanagement of spending, expenses, and income. When there is no budget, it is easy for the *outgo to exceed the income.* And when this happens, financial distress is soon to follow.

———— • • • ————

Nothing is cheap which is superfluous, for what one does not need, is dear at a penny.

Plutarch

———— • • • ————

Sometimes major life events can cause our credit card debt to get out of hand. A divorce or separation can play havoc on financial wellness. Two people who have been living under one roof must now support two households. Credit card shopping can buy new furniture for an apartment, new clothes for a new beau, entertainment to assuage our emotional pain, or even just "revenge buying" to act out our anger.

Catastrophes also can cause our credit card debt to mushroom beyond our ability to pay it off. For example, a medical emergency can not only create bills, but it can also create gaps in our income from lost work time. A major house or automobile repair can cost us thousands of dollars, and this never seems to happen at a good time. Our ancestors may have "saved for a rainy day," but if we have been following the guidance of our national leaders, then we probably have not even saved for a "partially cloudy day."

Another "final straw" for many credit card junkies is the unexpected job layoff. In these uncertain financial times many people who once felt they had job security have now discovered that even major corporations have a limit to how much red ink they can tolerate. Job losses or cuts in pay may occur in any industry, wrecking the finances of a household. When this happens, the strategy of charging on one credit card to pay off another soon becomes untenable.

———— • • • ————

A person who can't pay, gets another person who can't pay, to guarantee that he can pay.

Charles Dickens

———— • • • ————

When the House of Credit Cards Comes Tumbling Down

A married couple had the "honor" of being on the Phil Donahue show because they had a $52,900 debt spread over *sixty-two* active credit cards. Before 1980 they had no credit cards. Then the husband started graduate school and was sent a preapproved credit card. Soon the family needed one or two extra credit cards for family emergencies. The cards began to represent security to the couple. But it was a false security. Even though they were at limit on the cards, they were being sent more and more cards. Eventually they owed $4,000 a month just in credit card debt. They dreaded every payday. They paid on the cards with late notices first. Then they borrowed money on other cards to help pay the overdue cards. Restless nights and days became the norm. Finally, the "house of cards" came tumbling down when the wife had a medical emergency, leaving her unable to work for two months.

With counseling and a financial plan, their debt has been paid. And all but one credit card has been cut up and destroyed. In the process, the family has grown closer, the children have helped control expenses and learned the value of money, and the wife has become an expert at comparison shopping, bargain hunting and using coupons. The husband reflected that it took four years to get into debt and four years to get out of debt, and they had little to show for their heartache. The wife said that they now have more time together as a family and spend more time talking, playing games, and being with their children.

———•••———

Sometimes the best gain is to lose.
George Herbert

———•••———

Rules for Successful "Plastic Surgery"

Rule Number One:

Completely audit your credit card debt and your income to discover how much you actually owe and are spending to service your debt. From this you get the foundation for a budget and debt-repayment plan.

———•••———

Credit is like a looking-glass, which when once sullied by a breath, may be wiped clear again; but if once cracked can never be repaired.
Sir Walter Scott

———•••———

Rule Number Two:

Cut up all but one credit card. Shop for a card with a low monthly interest rate and low annual fee. Pay off all your other credit cards with the new lower-rate card's cash advance, and then consistently pay off the new card. You may go from paying 21 percent non-deductible interest to 14 percent non-deductible interest.

———•••———

Remember that credit is money.
Benjamin Franklin

———••——

Rule Number Three:

Decide your most vulnerable areas of spending (for example, shopping for clothes, eating out for lunch) and avoid these situations by either not going, or by not taking your credit card with you.

———••——

Buying on trust is the way to pay double.

———••——

Rule Number Four:

Establish a limit on impulse buying. Decide that you and your spouse will discuss any purchase over a set amount (for example, $25 or $50) before making the purchase.

———••——

Before you consult your fancy, consult your purse.
Benjamin Franklin

———••——

Rule Number Five:

Give each member of your household a cash allowance that can be for anything, but when it's gone there is no more until the next allowance day.

———••——

No man's credit is as good as his money.
Ed Howe

———••——

Rule Number Six:

Consider a brown-bag lunch program to cut your weekly food costs. Learn to use coupons for groceries, dinners out, or entertainment.

• • •

The surest way to establish your credit is to work yourself into the position of not needing any.

Maurice Switzer

• • •

Rule Number Seven:

Stop paying for lunch and dinner for your friends with your credit card, even if they pay you back in cash. You will spend the cash and have nothing to show for it but the bill from the credit card company at the end of the month.

• • •

Never spend your money before you have it.

Thomas Jefferson

• • •

Rule Number Eight:

Make your credit card purchases a line item in your monthly budget, and don't exceed it.

• • •

Youth is in danger until it learns to look upon debts as furies.

Edward G. Bulwer-Lytton

• • •

Rule Number Nine:

Rediscover life's simple pleasures by going to museums, libraries, zoos, the lake or beach, playing games with friends and family, having gatherings for special video tapes, and the like.

— • • • —

He that is of the opinion money will do everything may well be suspected of doing everything for money.
Benjamin Franklin

— • • • —

Rule Number Ten:

Begin a savings plan. Once you are in recovery from your credit card addiction, you can substitute a positive addiction by watching your savings grow. Buy a savings bond every time you deposit your pay check at the bank, or if your company has a payroll savings plan, use it.

— • • • —

'Tis against some men's principle to pay interest, and seems against others' interest to pay the principal.
Benjamin Franklin

— • • • —

CHAPTER NINE

The Power of Prepaying Your Mortgage

What do most homeowners in America have in common? They almost always pay too much for their mortgages. Over the course of a thirty-year mortgage you will pay approximately $330,000 for a $100,000 home. You are paying $230,000 just in interest! Only ten out of one hundred homeowners attempt to prepay their mortgages. Prepaying mortgages can be confusing and is rarely explained to the consumer when buying a home, for obvious reasons.

Let's not confuse prepaying a mortgage with taking out a fifteen-year loan instead of a thirty-year mortgage. Many people feel compelled to put themselves into a fifteen-year mortgage, which has a larger payment, when they cannot afford the increased monthly payments. When going into a fifteen-year mortgage, the homeowner has lost the flexibility to alter payments if necessary to offset unexpected expenses or emergencies.

However by taking out a thirty-year mortgage, the homeowner is now in the driver's seat and in control of monthly prepayment. Let's ask ourselves if it makes sense to prepay a mortgage. In our opinion, it almost always is to our advantage.

Let's look at some of the reasons. For explanation purposes, we are going to use a $100,000 mortgage at 10.5 percent interest rate. The biggest reason for prepaying the mortgage is interest savings. A $100,000 mortgage principal will hardly be touched for the first twenty-four years. Therefore, interest is what is being paid. The last six years is where most of the principal is paid. The total payment on a $100,000 thirty-year mortgage is approximately $329,000. Our interest in this example is $229,000, which represents 200+ percent of our original loan amount.

It is very important when buying a home on a thirty-year mortgage that you make sure there are no prepayment penalties. Many mortgage companies used to charge prepayment penalties if you increased the principal payments on a home.

On a $100,000 mortgage at 10.5 percent interest rate for thirty years, the consumer can save over $90,000 by paying approximately an extra $85 a month prepayment. In addition, the mortgage will be paid off in twenty years. All this by paying an extra $2.80 per day toward your principal! See "Table of a Typical $100,000 Thirty Year Mortgage."

The Disadvantage of the Thirty-Year Mortgage

Notice in the chart above that after paying on your mortgage for ten years, you have paid more in interest than the original loan principal. However, you still owe $91,622.16. So whistle and sing, "I owe, I owe, it's off to work I go."

Table of a Typical $100,000 Thirty Year Mortgage

Year Number	Total Payment Amount	Total Interest Paid	Total Principal Paid	Loan Balance
1	10,976.88	10,476.36	500.52	99,499.48
2	21,953.76	20,897.56	1,056.20	98,943.80
3	32,930.64	31,257.53	1,673.11	98,326.89
4	43,907.52	41,549.49	2,358.03	97,641.97
5	54,884.40	51,766.01	3,118.39	96,881.61
6	65,861.28	61,898.73	3,962.55	96,037.45
7	76,838.16	71,938.41	4,899.75	95,100.25
8	87,815.01	81,874.81	5,940.23	94,059.77
9	98,791.92	91,696.53	7,095.39	92,904.61
10	**109,768.80**	**101,390.96**	**8,377.84**	**91,622.16**
15	164,653.20	147,404.73	17,248.47	82,751.53
20	219,537.30	187,327.90	32,209.70	67,790.30
25	274,422.00	216,978.67	57,443.33	42,556.67
30	**329,304.00**	**229,304.00**	**100,000.00**	**0.00**

If you decide to increase your payment, you will pay off your loan much faster. In the example that we have been using, the monthly payment was $914.74. If you were to increase this payment by only $85.26 per month, or $2.80 per day, you would receive the benefits shown in the following table.

Table of Benefits of Prepaying Your Mortgage an Extra $85.26 Per Month

Year Number	Annual Payment Amount	Annual Interest Paid	Annual Principal Paid	Loan Balance
1	12,000.00	10,425.66	1,574.34	98,425.66
2	12,000.00	10,252.18	1,747.82	96,677.84
3	12,000.00	10,059.54	1,940.46	94,737.38
4	12,000.00	9,854.72	2,154.28	92,583.10
5	12,000.00	9,608.28	2,391.72	90,191.38
6	12,000.00	9,344.72	2,655.28	87,536.10
7	12,000.00	9,052.10	2,947.90	84,688.20
8	12,000.00	8,727.23	3,272.77	81,315.43
9	12,000.00	8,366.58	3,633.42	77,682.01
10	12,000.00	7,966.16	4,033.84	73,648.17
11	12,000.00	7,521.60	4,478.40	69,169.77
12	12,000.00	7,028.07	4,971.93	64,197.84
13	12,000.00	6,480.15	5,519.85	58,766.99
14	12,000.00	5,871.84	6,128.16	52,549.83
15	12,000.00	5,196.48	6,803.52	45,746.31
16	12,000.00	4,446.72	7,553.28	38,193.03
17	12,000.00	3,614.33	8,385.67	29,807.36
18	12,000.00	2,690.18	9,309.82	20,497.54
19	12,000.00	1,664.22	10,335.78	10,161.76
20	10,689.65	527.89	10,161.76	0.00
	Cumulative Payments	Cumulative Interest Paid	Cumulative Principal Paid	
	238,689.65	**138,689.65**	**100,000.00**	

Save Your Interest Payments to Use for Investments

If you pay your mortgage in thirty years, you will have a home. If you prepay your mortgage in twenty years, you will have a home and ten years to invest money in short- and long-term investments for your retirement. You get this benefit by only paying an extra $85.26 per month, or $2.80 per day.

If you invest in mutual funds and get an average rate of return of 10 percent, then your money will double in approximately seven years. Mutual funds have averaged approximately 15 percent annually over the last fifteen years. You should be able to expect at least a 10 percent return on your investment if you are patient and stay with your chosen investments.

How to Turn Your House Payment into a House, Plus $206,552 in Cash

If, after paying off your mortgage in twenty years, you choose to invest the monthly amount you would have spent on your mortgage payment, then you will not only own your house but, at the end of thirty years, will own a substantial nest egg. Look at the table below to see how your $1,000 monthly payment can now be turned into retirement money. See "Investment Table for Savings from Prepayment" chart on next page.

How to Structure Your Prepayments

You can spend very little money and get an amortization schedule to help you prepay your mortgage. You can also pay your accountant to devise a schedule for you.

Investment Table for Savings from Prepayment

Year Number	Annual Investment	Average Rate of Return	Total Principal and Earnings
1	12,000.00	10%	12,670.28
2	12,000.00	10%	26,667.31
3	12,000.00	10%	42,130.00
4	12,000.00	10%	59,211.85
5	12,000.00	10%	78,082.38
6	12,000.00	10%	98,928.91
7	12,000.00	10%	121,958.34
8	12,000.00	10%	147,399.25
9	12,000.00	10%	175,504.16
10	12,000.00	10%	**206,552.02**

However, there may be confusion if you don't keep a close eye on how your payments are posted at the bank or mortgage company. Clerks make mistakes, and sometimes your payment is not deducted from the principal. Mortgages are often sold to different lenders, and this adds room for more confusion. You still have a borrower's right of prepayment. You can specifically request that your mortgage company accept payments against your principal and dismiss all future charges of interest against the amount you prepaid.

If you need help in devising your personal mortgage prepayment schedule, please contact us at Mind Over Money, Inc. We can help you find a product that will serve your needs the best.

Shop for the Best Mortgage Rate and Be Prepared to Refinance

Another important tool in the arena of financial wellness is learning the benefits of lower mortgage rates and refinancing. If you have a thirty-year mortgage at 10.5 percent, you have already seen that it will cost you $329,304 for a $100,000 house. What if you refinanced a $100,000 house at a lower rate of 8 percent interest? Would you save much money? The answer is a definite yes. Let's look at some numbers with the hypothetical assumption that you have thirty years to pay off $100,000 at 8 percent, instead of 10.5 percent.

Table of a $100,000 Thirty Year Mortgage at 8 Percent Interest

Year Number	Annual Payment Total	Annual Interest Paid	Annual Principal Paid	Loan Balance
1	8,805.12	7,969.82	835.30	99,164.70
2	8,805.12	7,900.49	904.63	98,260.07
3	8,805.12	7,825.40	979.72	97,280.35
4	8,805.12	7,744.09	1,061.03	96,219.32
5	8,805.12	7,656.01	1,149.11	95,070.21
6	8,805.12	7,560.63	1,244.49	93,825.72
7	8,805.12	7,457.35	1,347.77	92,477.95
8	8,805.12	7,345.48	1,459.64	91,018.31
9	8,805.12	7,224.33	1,580.79	89,437.52
10	8,805.12	7,093.12	1,712.00	87,725.52
15	8,805.12	6,254.54	2,550.58	76,783.19
20	8,805.12	5,005.12	3,800.00	60,480.67
25	8,805.12	3,143.70	5,661.42	36,192.49
30	**8,805.12**	**370.50**	**8,441.49**	**0.00**
	Cumulative Total Payments	Cumulative Interest Paid	Cumulative Principal Paid	
	264,160.47	164,160.47	100,000.00	

You can see from the table above that if you had the 8 percent lower rate of interest, instead of 10.5 percent, and paid your house off in the full thirty years, you would save more than $65,000. Wouldn't you rather have the $65,000 for your retirement instead of giving it to your bank or mortgage lender? You get that $65,000 without even the benefit you would derive if you also used our prepayment arrangements. Look at the table below to see the advantage of both a lower interest rate and increased payments to prepay principal.

Table of Prepayment Schedule ($1,000 Per Month) and Lower Interest (8%) Benefits

Year Number	Annual Payments	Annual Interest Paid	Annual Principal Paid	Loan Balance
1	12,000.00	7,850.05	4,149.95	95,850.05
2	12,000.00	7,505.58	4,494.42	91,355.63
3	12,000.00	7,132.55	4,867.45	86,488.18
4	12,000.00	6,728.55	5,271.45	81,216.73
5	12,000.00	6,291.00	5,709.00	75,507.73
6	12,000.00	5,817.18	6,182.82	69,324.91
7	12,000.00	5,304.01	6,695.99	62,628.92
8	12,000.00	4,748.25	7,251.75	55,377.17
9	12,000.00	4,146.35	7,853.65	47,523.52
10	12,000.00	3,494.51	8,505.49	39,018.03
11	12,000.00	2,788.56	9,211.44	29,806.59
12	12,000.00	2,024.00	9,976.00	19,830.59
13	12,000.00	1,196.00	10,804.00	9,026.59
14	9,341.34	314.75	9,026.59	0.00
	Total Payments	Total Interest	Total Principal	
	165,341.34	**65,341.34**	**100,000.00**	

If you did both the refinancing and the prepayment of principal by increasing your monthly payment to $1,000, then you would have paid off your house in fourteen years. If you decided to invest the monthly $1,000 at 10 percent for the remainder of the thirty years that you were going to pay on your house anyway, then you would have sixteen years to be building a nest egg for retirement. The following table will show you how much you would have in that nest egg, in addition to a paid-off house.

Investment Table for Savings from Prepaying a 30 Year Mortgage in 20 Years and Refinancing to a Lower Interest Rate and Interest Savings

Year Number	Annual Investment	Average Annual Interest Rate	Total Principal and Earnings
1	12,000.00	10%	12,670.28
2	12,000.00	10%	26,667.31
3	12,000.00	10%	42,130.00
4	12,000.00	10%	59,211.85
5	12,000.00	10%	78,082.38
6	12,000.00	10%	98,928.91
7	12,000.00	10%	121,958.34
8	12,000.00	10%	147,399.25
9	12,000.00	10%	175,504.16
10	12,000.00	10%	206,552.02
11	12,000.00	10%	240,851.00
12	12,000.00	10%	278,741.53
13	12,000.00	10%	320,599.69
14	12,000.00	10%	366,840.94
15	12,000.00	10%	417,924.27
16	12,000.00	10%	**474,356.68**

After paying off your mortgage in fourteen years by refinancing at a lower interest rate and making monthly payments of $1,000 to prepay your principal, you can choose to invest the monthly amount you would have spent on your mortgage payments. Then, you not only own your house, but at the end of the thirty years you have $474,356.68 in cash. Review the table above to see how your $1,000 monthly payment can now be turned into retirement money. You can see that you have now turned your monthly payments into a paid-off house and nearly a half million dollars!

CHAPTER TEN

Budgets and Cash Flow Statements: The Tools to Prevent "Too Much Month at the End of the Money"

What does an organized cash flow statement mean to you? An organized cash flow statement means that you can and should write down every source of money that you receive annually. This could be child support, rental income, interest income, or employment income. Once you know the total of all income, it makes your direction clear as you plunge ahead in your financial life.

The budget cannot work if we do not know the total resources we have to spend. It would be impossible for any company to plan its annual budget if it did not know what its financial resources were.

A helpful hint for preparing a cash flow statement is to write down all sources of annual income and divide by twelve, to calculate a monthly budget. Even though you may receive the money annually, quarterly, or semi-annually, reducing the income to monthly will allow a safety check against the monthly budget. We are not dealing with reality if during some months we have a large surplus and feel that we can go ahead and spend the money.

Example of Income, Taxes and Cash Flow Statement

Taxable Income	Monthly	Annually
Salary (client)	$3,916	$47,000
Salary (spouse)	$2,333	$28,000
Interest Income		
Stock Dividends		
Pensions		
Alimony		
Bonus Income		
Non-Taxable Income		
Social Security		
Child Support		
Municipal Bonds		
Total Income	**$6,249**	**$75,000**
Taxes Due		
Federal Income Tax (client)	$989	$11,868
Federal Income Tax (spouse)	$583	$6,936
State Income Tax (client)		
State Income Tax (spouse)		
FICA/Self-Employment Tax (client)	$313	$3,756
FICA/Self-Employment Tax (spouse)	$187	$2,244
Tax Totals	**$2,072**	**$25,664**
Total Monthly Income	**$6,249**	
Less Total Monthly Taxes	**($2,072)**	
Net Monthly Cash Flow	**$4,177**	

Use the form on the following page to discover your personal income, taxes, and cash flow statement. Fill out the income categories. Then fill out your estimated federal income taxes based on 17 percent for the range of $1 to $35,799; 28 percent for the range $35,800 to $86,499; and 31 percent for the range $86,500 income and above. Your estimated FICA and Medicare taxes are based on a rate of 7.65 percent of your income. Then subtract the total taxes from your total income to determine your net cash flow. See "Example of Income, Taxes, and Cash Flow Statement" chart on the following page.

Budget Planning

What do a large corporation, a small business, a church, a civic organization, and a family have in common? They all spend money monthly and must have a budget of monthly expenses and a monitoring of cash flow. Many people tell us, "I don't have a budget and I don't need one to operate." This is true. It is not necessary to have a budget to operate, unless you want to do so efficiently. What we really hear them saying is that they do not want to take the time to organize and discipline themselves, or they do not know *how* to budget.

To amplify the point for a second, think about trying to build a DC-10 or interstate highway without a blueprint, strategy, or goals. We are sure something could be built, but would the quality be there or would it last for long? We doubt it. Let's look at why a budget is necessary and how to create one.

My Personal Income, Taxes, and Cash Flow Statement

Taxable Income	Monthly	Annually
Salary (client)		
Salary (spouse)		
Interest Income		
Stock Dividends		
Pensions		
Alimony		
Bonus Income		
Non-Taxable Income		
Social Security		
Child Support		
Municipal Bonds		
Total Income		
Taxes Due		
Federal Income Tax (client)		
Federal Income Tax (spouse)		
State Income Tax (client)		
State Income Tax (spouse)		
FICA/Medicare/ Self-Employment Tax (client)		
FICA/Medicare/ Self-Employment Tax (spouse)		
Tax Totals		
Total Monthly Income		
Less Total Monthly Taxes	( )	
Net Monthly Cash Flow		

If a person plans to retire, save money, make invest-ments, purchase life insurance, etc., he must know two things. First, what are the various sources of total monthly income? Examples of income are wages, inter-est, dividends, rental collections, and pension. Second, after establishing all of the sources of income, what are the expenses it takes to survive monthly? These expenses will range from house payments and rent to buying toothpaste. Here lies the problem (and this is the reason many do not have budgets): Most people never take the time to analyze what is happening month to month.

It is important to budget an amount of money for such things as credit cards, groceries, gasoline, dog grooming, and miscellaneous expenses such as toothpaste and shampoo. A budget must also make allowances for cash spending money, as well as for the obvious house and car note. It makes good sense that a person needs to know where he or she is at in their present financial situation before they can know where they're headed.

This leads us to the point of why a budget is so neces-sary. One must know each month if their basic and nec-essary expenses are exceeding, equal to, or less than their income. This is mandatory in order to know what sur-plus, if any, is left each month to do financial planning. Remember that financial planning is a generic term that can apply to balancing a budget, having a savings ac-count, preparing for education needs, and preparing for retirement.

— • • • —

It isn't how much we make; it's what we do with it that counts.

— • • • —

The Components of a Budget

A budget should be divided into three major areas. Let's analyze these three sections of the budget and come up with some helpful hints that will keep us out of trouble.

Fixed Expenses

Examples of fixed debt are cars, homes, or insurance. These are necessary debts and will, for the most part, remain the same each month.

Make a list of all fixed debt. A goal for financial wellness is to keep fixed debt at 50 percent or less of your monthly income. Take those fixed expenses like car insurance or taxes that we pay quarterly, semi-annually, or annually, and divide them into monthly installment payments. This will give you a true monthly overhead and eliminate those surprise bills. You may be asking yourself, Where do I put the money until the bill is due? This money should be placed in a short-term Money Market Account to serve as a holding tank until the quarterly or semi-annual bill is due.

Variable Expenses

Such things as groceries, medical bills, household utilities, and clothing are variable expenses. When dealing with these budget items, we must be careful that we have accounted for all fixed debt first to determine what we have left to spend on variable expenses. These are certainly necessary items, but most of us don't have a clue of what we spent per year or per month on them. The best way to approach this problem is to go back through your checkbook for the past six months and add your checks together in these basic categories. If you charged all your clothes, doctor bills, or household needs, add your checks payable to charge cards into the total. Once you have a total, divide by the number of months (six), and you have now broken your expenses into a monthly number that you can *realistically* budget.

Notice we said *realistically*. If this number is not realistic, it will be of no value in budget planning. That is why we go back to the checkbook register.

This brings us to the third area, Miscellaneous Expenses. Many people will look in their checkbooks after paying fixed or variable expenses and—if they have money left—feel they can spend this surplus in the miscellaneous category.

Well, it's easy to see why this theory can blow up in our faces: We have not allowed for upcoming payments that are due on a non-monthly basis, such as quarterly insurance or a large medical bill that comes unexpectedly.

Tithing

Some people will want to include a section for tithing in their monthly budget. Whether a person chooses to tithe a percentage of their gross income or a percentage of their net income is strictly a personal matter.

There are many different approaches to tithing. Some people choose to pay a tithe in one lump sum at the beginning or end of the calendar year. Some pay at the start or finish of their fiscal year. Others pay by the week or by the month. If you are unable to write a large check at one time, practice the discipline of setting aside a percentage of each paycheck and giving once per pay period. Allocate that amount first when your check comes in. By so doing, you will be less likely to "rob the tithe" for other reasons.

If you have considered tithing, but have never practiced it, talk to someone who does. We've never met anyone who regrets it.

Miscellaneous Expenses

The third type of expense is miscellaneous in which we place charge cards for vacations, Christmas, birthdays, and sporting equipment. This is not to say that all of these expenses are bad, but these are the areas where most people tend to get into trouble. This is the area where we can get into trouble *especially* if there is no budget at all. If we have done a good job in the first two areas of our budget, it will become clear what we can spend. We now know if the new bass boat or diamond ring or vacation to Hawaii or new furniture for the house is an affordable expense.

We must be careful in the miscellaneous area not to say, "Charge it," because *we only have left whatever is left.* What's left will not be enough to pay the credit cards if we spread it out over five credit cards, then run the cards to the limit for miscellaneous items.

Emergency Cash Funds for Your Budget

To many of us, an emergency cash fund means to grab a credit card when something unexpected comes up! However, real funds of emergency cash should equal three months of the expenses that it takes to run our budgets. The best way to build an emergency fund is to take approximately 5 percent of our take-home pay and place it into a separate interest-bearing account. Over a period of time you will have quite an accumulation. We know that the car will break down, the washer will go out, or one of the children will break a limb.

Most people in our country do not have a cash fund set up, but it is a must for financial wellness. As we stated earlier, charging everything on a credit card would simply add to the monthly overhead. This would also take a major toll on your cash flow. Once the cash accumulates in your emergency cash fund to where it equals your expenses for three months, then we can move into short-term investment strategy.

The Cost of Using Retirement Funds for Emergencies

Dave and Sue came into our office with a real dilemma. The engine had gone out in Dave's work truck and was going to cost $1,500 to repair. They only had $300 in savings, but they had put $1,500 into an IRA at a local bank two years before. When talking to the bank about a loan, the bank did not want to grant one without collateral and would not use retirement money as collateral. Dave was informed that he could withdraw the $1,500 from his IRA, but would pay $150 tax penalty plus 25 percent tax at the time of withdrawal. This would be an additional $150 plus $375. This forced Dave into having to withdraw $1,500 for the car repair and pay $525 worth of penalties. This is the reason for having an operating emergency cash fund before putting money into Qualified Retirement Planning. The car repair was $1,500, but it cost Dave and Sue $2,025 because they used their retirement funds for emergency funds.

The Changing Nature of Budgets

We must always keep in mind that the budget is not etched in stone. It is a guideline that should be followed very closely. If modification needs to be made in certain areas, then make such adjustments. However, most people feel you should spend the money and use a budget to keep score of expenses. But the budget is not a scoring tool; it is a guideline that should be followed. When money is gone in an area, it means it is no longer available, and we should quit spending in that area.

REMEMBER: The Budget is Life's Financial Blueprint

Without a budget there is:

1. No sense of spending habits
2. No record of actual expenses
3. No planning process/no direction
4. No "checks & balances" with yourself
5. No hope for financial success over the long term

Budgets Make Good "Cents"

We have spent a lot of time on budgets in this material, but there is a need to have this foundation. Without the budget in written form, there is no strategy. Let's analyze the way a budget should be set. The following sample is a budget for you to begin to fill out!

So many people we work with today do not understand why their spending is out of control like a ship in a typhoon. Complete your personal budget and take the helm of your own ship. Use your budget to steer away from the hidden rocks and narrow straits of your financial life. The world is yours to sail if you just have a chart to guide your way!

———•••———

If you always do what you always did, you'll always get what you always got.

———•••———

Example of a Monthly Budget

FIXED EXPENSES	BUDGETED AMOUNT
PERSONAL EXPENSES	
HOUSING:	
Mortgage/Rent	$750
Property Taxes	$150
Homeowners Insurance	$80
Homeowners Dues	$20
Maintenance Dues	$40
Utilities	$200
TRANSPORTATION:	
Car Payments	$350
Car Insurance	$100
Gas	$150
Maintenance	$50
License/Fees	$5
Fixed Expenses Subtotal	**$1895**
VARIABLE EXPENSES	
Personal Expenses:	
Food & Beverage	$400
Clothing	$100
Furnishings	$20
Personal Care/Cash	$200
Medical/Dental/Drugs	$100
Medical Insurance	$250
Life/Disability Insurance	$100
Education/Self-improvement	$50
Variable Expenses Subtotal	**$1220**
Fixed + Variable Expenses = Subtotal	**$3115**
EMERGENCY CASH FUND (Goal is to build up to equal three times your fixed and variable totals)	
Emergency Fund Contribution	$200
MISCELLANEOUS EXPENSES	
Entertainment and Gifts	$100
Vacation & Holidays	$150
Church	$150
Charitable Contributions	$50
Child Care	$250
Miscellaneous	$100
Miscellaneous Expenses Subtotal	$1,000
GRAND TOTAL OF EXPENSES	**$4115**
TOTAL INCOME FROM CASH FLOW (PAGE 112)	**$4177**
REMAINING INCOME FOR INVESTMENTS	**$62**

My Personal Monthly Budget

FIXED EXPENSES	BUDGETED AMOUNT
PERSONAL EXPENSES	
HOUSING:	
Mortgage/Rent	
Property Taxes	
Homeowners Insurance	
Homeowners Dues	
Maintenance Dues	
Utilities	
TRANSPORTATION:	
Car Payments	
Car Insurance	
Gas	
Maintenance	
License/Fees	
Fixed Expenses Subtotal	
VARIABLE EXPENSES	
Personal Expenses:	
Food & Beverage	
Clothing	
Furnishings	
Personal Care/Cash	
Medical/Dental/Drugs	
Medical Insurance	
Life/Disability Insurance	
Education/Self-improvement	
Variable Expenses Subtotal	
Fixed + Variable Expenses = Subtotal	
EMERGENCY CASH FUND (Goal is to build up to equal three times your fixed and variable totals)	
Emergency Fund Contribution	
MISCELLANEOUS EXPENSES	
Entertainment and Gifts	
Vacation & Holidays	
Church	
Charitable Contrivbutions	
Child Care	
Miscellaneous	
Miscellaneous Expenses Subtotal	
GRAND TOTAL OF EXPENSES	
TOTAL INCOME FROM CASH FLOW (PAGE 112)	
REMAINING INCOME FOR INVESTMENTS	

CHAPTER ELEVEN

Medical Insurance Planning

You will surely say this proverb to Me, "Physician, heal yourself! Whatever we have heard done in Capernaum, do also here in Your country."

Luke 4:23

— • • • —

Our country is in a health care crisis the likes of which we have never known before. Medical costs continue to escalate so that at times even the physicians themselves cannot afford to heal their families. Hospitalization insurance is what we all need in order to stay out of the poorhouse, but it is often misunderstood. We constantly hear inaccuracies about premiums and coverage on group and individual medical insurance policies.

The most common complaint is that medical insurance premiums are rising. And all of us want to know where it will end. Many people say, "We're headed for socialized medicine." We hope not, because as bad as the insurance companies appear to be on this subject, if you like your present Social Security system, you will *love* government-controlled insurance. Let's analyze how group and individual medical insurance policies compare and look for some of the pitfalls.

Group Insurance Policies

Group insurance comes in a lot of flavors, but most plans have a front-end annual deductible and pay 80 percent of the first $5,000 of medical expenses. After reaching this $5,000 expense, most good plans will go to 100 percent of usual and customary expenses, not to exceed a lifetime maximum of either $1 million, $2 million, or no limit, depending on the policy. These plans are called comprehensive major medical policies.

BEWARE! You cannot shop medical policies based on cost only! As a matter of fact, if a salesperson tells you his plan is the cheapest, run for the hills.This usually means one of the following things: First, there is probably a six-month rate guarantee or no rate guarantee, which means your rates may be going up soon. Second, there are pre-existing condition limitations, which means a recurrence of an illness will not be covered. Or third, the claims service is just plain lousy.

One of the authors of this book broke his back in a bicycle accident and within one year his premiums had gone from $350 per month to $1,550 per month. Obviously he dropped the policy. In finding a new policy, he began to study more closely the companies and policies. One company's proposal seemed a good policy at a fair price. However, when researching the company's assets, he discovered they had a total of $130,000 in assets. One policyholder alone could bankrupt the company if a catastrophic illness occurred.

The ideal cost plan to look for in medical insurance is this: Comprehensive major medical with $250 or $500 annual deductible per calendar year that will pay 80 percent of the first $5,000 and 100 percent thereafter to an unlimited major medical limit. Also look for a one-year rate guarantee.

Consider a pre-certified group plan. This allows one to save premium dollars by calling ahead and letting the insurance company know the nature of the pending treatment. This may allow the insurance company to monitor your treatment more closely so that the hospital does not overcharge you.

In the group insurance market there are many good companies selling medical insurance, but few do a good job of service after the sell. Make sure that you only deal with an A or A+ company rating from the "Best Review," the bible of the insurance business.

Individual Medical Insurance Policies

Individual medical insurance policies, if they are good plans, will work identically like the description we have given on group plans. The problem in the marketplace is that for every plan that has the comprehensive benefits there are ten others that do not and are filled with exclusions and limitations. If you are not a trained insurance person, chances are you will make a mistake, especially if only shopping for a bargain policy. One of the common problems related to this in today's market is the plan that states you have a $200 or $300 deductible and the plan will then pay 100 percent up to $1,000,000. Our question is always, *100 percent of what?* The answer is hard to find as you look deep into the contract's list of exclusions that are not covered.

There are two other types of policies, which can be called comprehensive major medical—First, the HMO,

PPO, or managed care plans. These plans tend to be less expensive. They are health maintenance organizations (HMO) or preferred provider plans (PPO) designed for controlled access to health care. Some plans scrutinize all services and manage your treatment. They may offer a list of hospitals, clinics, pharmacies, and doctors that the policyholder must use. If the policyholder uses them, he or she can save premium dollars and get more of the health care bills paid with a minimal deductible per visit. The disadvantage of these plans is that you lose your freedom to choose your own doctor, some services may be limited, and to date there has been no demonstrable savings on most services because the administration and management costs of the HMO, PPO, and managed care often exceed any savings. What has been created is a new industry: the management of medical care.

The second type of policy is the standard comprehensive medical plan. This plan does not limit the choice of doctor or institution but usually has higher premiums, front-end annual deductibles, and 80 percent coverage up to $5,000. In the future, the managed care plans and standard plans will probably be combined in some form to protect the consumer from excessive charges from inpatient services and other medical care that has caused the current health care crisis.

A Word About Mental Health Claims

One of the important areas of financial wellness is understanding the medical industry as it relates to mental health and insurance companies. Our country is scrutinizing all areas of the health care-insurance company relationship, especially mental health reimbursement. Traditionally insurance companies have reimbursed health care so that practitoners are rewarded for placing patients into hospitals. Outpatient health care would be reimbursed at 50 percent to 80 percent, while inpatient coverage was 100 percent. Mental health benefits were often even more limited, with outpatient therapy either not paid for at all, limited to $25 per session, or paid at 50 percent per session.

The American Academy of Family Physicians has estimated that approximately 75 percent of all health care needs are somehow related to mental health, stress, or lifestyle. We seek to find physical causes and medical cures for a variety of psychosomatic or stress-related problems. We live chronically dysfunctional lives of "struggling for the legal tender" and deficit spending, and yet we are rewarded and feel somehow comforted if our high blood pressure, ulcers, aches and pains are "physical."

Our health care insurance industry has developed around the premise that if a problem is physical, it will pay your physician handsomely to fix it. You may get great reimbursement for a $100,000 hospital bill for by-pass surgery, but your policy may not cover the stop-smoking program, cardiac rehabilitation exercise program, heart healthy nutrition classes, stress management or financial wellness programs at all because they are preventions and not treatments. Contrast a $25 reimbursement payment for 50 to 60 minutes of outpatient psychotherapy with the reimbursement payment of $5,000 hospital charges and $5,000 surgeon charges for 50 to 60 minutes of day surgery, and it becomes easy to see how business interests in the health care industry lead to emphasis on treatments that will create financial wellness for the institution and not necessarily for the patient.

The differential in reimbursing for health care created a situation in our country where people needing medical help might often seek more expensive care because the reimbursement was better. This led to abuse and the birth of more hospitals, which in turn led to a symbiotic relationship between health care providers and hospitals. Pressure to keep hospital beds filled and better inpatient reimbursement contributed to more people being hospitalized. Now the nation is reeling under runaway health costs, and we are trying to contain them by managed health care plans, preferred provider organizations and health maintenance organizations.

Most health insurance policies will now have a lifetime cap on mental health claims of anywhere from 10,000 to 30,000 dollars. Since the average daily cost of a mental health institution is approximately 1,000 dollars, even with a high level of coverage a person will have 30 days to regain mental health. This leads us to a crucial point—"the system."

The need for mental health treatment results from one or more psychological, behavioral or lifestyle problems. Patients may be suffering from depression, anxiety, or any number of substance-abuse issues. Often, these conditions are rooted in low self-esteem or family issues.

During treatment in many psychiatric institutions, a patient receives little training in the area of total wellness—stress issues, food, money, etc. The emphasis is put on medicating and tranquilizing away the inner despair and anxiety from our problems with managing money, communicating with our families, or coping with stress. The irony here is that many people who are under psychiatric care are experiencing stress over money issues—most either have too much money or not enough.

According to a leading drug and alcohol rehabilitation group, many people tend to gain weight after release from a drug or alcohol treatment facility. What is happening? Are we teaching people to trade addictions and working on symptoms instead of dealing with core based problems and issues? Institutions often do not train patients in areas of mental wellness such as money, nutrition, exercise, and the positive aspects of play for two reasons. First, they do not have a properly trained staff in these areas. Second, they do not know how to get insurance company reimbursement in these areas. It is easier to get paid for medicating people's pain from dysfunctional lifestyles and habits than to teach lifestyle changes.

When patients are admitted to these hospitals, they begin to take various drugs and attend classes and support groups. Many of these classes and group sessions are led by paraprofessionals—former drug and alcohol patients. Therefore, the patient is paying for professional care, but in many cases is minimally exposed to consulation by professional psychologists and psychiatrists. We are back to another financial issue because the paraprofessionals cost less to employ. If an employee works at $10 per hour conducting a group for 20 patients being charged $100 per hour for group "therapy," then a hospital makes $2,000 per hour from a $10 investment. If an insurance company will pay for these services only because the person is in the hospital, then there is motivation to use the more expensive inpatient intervention and the lesser trained staff.

The financial dynamics of our health care system are enough to make some people grab a credit card and go on a shopping spree. Hospitalized people who are unable to get to the mall often turn to another popular American coping tool—high fat foods. Patients often eat a lot while in the hospial working on their lifestyle stress and later in the day sit in their rooms and worry about how they will pay the balance of their hospital bill. Even if they are able to get a handle on their immediate concerns and problems, there are newfound stresses and problems being amplified by the institution.

Living within the "system," unfortunately, means that when the insurance runs out at 30 days or less, the patient is sent home. Is the patient well? No, but the institution does not want a patient with no more insurance coverage. Lack of quality help and sufficient dollars for mental health assistance in our country is an area that society does not recognize as a major problem.

Insurance companies do not treat mental illness as a real "medical claim issue" with the limits they place on claims. Hospitals and clinics have hurt themselves with insurance companies because of abuse and deception. Such abuses include hospital confinement for those who don't need it, the overuse of medication, and extended unnecessary hospital confinement for patients with good insurance. The patient and general public lose financially because patients cannot receive the thorough treatment necessary to make a lifestyle change when they desperately need it.

Unfortunately, we are caught in a vicious cycle of poor mental health. Many of us who probably need counseling cannot afford the assistance. This only causes more financial pressure for the future, because we do not get the help we need and continue to operate unhealthily at our jobs and with our families. This allows us to perpetuate the problem by passing it on to our children and then to future generations. Not only do we, as a society, pay "big bucks" for mental health care, patients pay a high price personally and emotionally when they don't receive adequate care. When insurance won't reimburse adequately for cost-effective, quality outpatient care, and patients pay less for more expensive inpatient care because of better reimbursement, then our American industries also pay a high price in lost productivity from

mentally distressed employees and higher insurance premiums from over-utilized, expensive inpatient treatments.

In closing, please remember that medical insurance
determinations cannot be solely judged by which carriers
have the cheapest premiums.

CHAPTER TWELVE

Financial Statements: The Answer to Net Worth

Many people ask us, "Why do I need a financial statement?" This is a good question, and hopefully the answer will become obvious.

A financial statement is a financial X-ray of a person's current economic situation. This statement gives a total picture of current financial condition as it relates to past financial decisions, current budget, cash flow, insurance, and most importantly, the present net worth of one's estate.

Most bankers count heavily on financial statements; it is usually the first thing that the banker wants to see when a customer requests a loan. Why does a family or a business need a financial statement? First and foremost, a banker will not make a loan to an individual or a company without a financial statement. The financial statement lets the lending officer know if assets are equal to, greater than, or less than one's liabilities.

The financial statement also allows the lending officer to determine how much, or what percentage, of one's assets are cash, mutual funds, stock, IRAs, or other liquid assets. Most bankers will be concerned if a financial statement consists of very few liquid assets or cash on hand.

This leads us to the second reason for such statements: It is important to know how much of the financial statement consists of nonliquid assets, or investments such as raw land, real estate, limited partnerships, mortgages, business interests, cars, boats, etc. Obviously these possessions are important, but there must be a proper balance between these assets and liquid assets.

One should pay close attention to the liabilities (debts owed) against these nonliquid assets. A bank loan officer will not give full market value credit for these assets. Therefore, liabilities against such assets must be kept to a minimum.

The third reason for a financial statement relates to our prior discussion about budgets, cash flow, and insurance. The financial statement allows the banker to see how income stacks up annually against outgoing expenses. A person would certainly not want to tell the lending officer he does not know what his expenses are, relative to his income. Please do not pass over this statement lightly. In recent years, banking institutions have begun to look more closely at the surplus monthly income of an individual in order to determine his or her ability to handle repayment of a loan.

Last, but not least, cash-value life insurance should be shown on a financial statement because it is a liquid asset that can be assigned to the bank as collateral. It is also important to note that a lending officer likes to see insurance that can be assigned to the bank, in the event of a death, to cover one's bank loan.

In closing, let's restate the reasons for a financial statement: As a person accrues financial possessions, it is important to keep score of liquid and nonliquid assets and the liabilities against those assets. When liabilities are deducted from assets, and the net assets are equal to or less than the liabilities, one has achieved zero net worth. In financial statements, the old cliché—"no pain, no gain"—is not necessarily true. Many people can work a lifetime under financial stress and pain, but by not adequately keeping score and by making bad financial decisions, they have no gain.

Financial Statement

		1. Assets (Market Value)	2. Liabilities
Very Low	Cash and Checking Accounts		
	T-Bills, Govt. Bonds & Money Market		
	Savings Accounts & CDs		
Low	Municipal Bonds/Funds		
	Corporate Bonds/Income Mutual Funds		
	Notes & Mortgages Receivables		
	Life Insurance Cash Value		
	Fixed Annuities		
Medium	IRA, Keogh, TSA, 401K Plans		
	Corporate Qualified Plans (vested)		
	Residence (Home)		
	Common or Preferred Stock		
	Capital Accumulation Mutual Funds		

	Growth Mutual Funds	_____	_____
	Variable Annuities	_____	_____
	Income Real Property	_____	_____
High	Undeveloped Land	_____	_____
	Real Estate Partnerships	_____	_____
	Energy Exploration Partnerships	_____	_____
	Equipment Lease, R & D, and Tax Shelters	_____	_____
	Business Interest	_____	_____
	Agriculture and Ranching	_____	_____
	Art, Antiques, Stamps, and Gems	_____	_____
	Gold, Silver, and Coins	_____	_____
Very High	Commodities/ Options	_____	_____
	Personal property/ Bequests	_____	_____
	Automobiles	_____	_____
	Recreational Property	_____	_____
	Other Loans & Liabilities	_____	_____
	(credit cards)	_____	_____
	TOTALS	**_____**	**_____**
	TOTALS	**_____**	(_____)

Subtract total liabilities (column 2) from market value (column 1) to determine your net worth.

$$\underset{\text{column 2 total}}{\underline{\hspace{3cm}}} - \underset{\text{column 1 total}}{\underline{\hspace{3cm}}} = \underset{\text{net worth}}{\underline{\hspace{3cm}}}$$

Evaluation: If your net worth is _____ percent above total liabilities, your score is: 10 percent or less = below standard; 11 to 20 percent = fair; 21 to 30 percent = average; 31 to 40 percent = above average; 41 to 50 percent = excellent.

CHAPTER THIRTEEN

Short- and Long-Term Investments

The Amateur Investor

Who is the amateur investor? Most of us in this country fit into this category. The large brokerage houses on Wall Street and the large insurance companies of our nation employ the experts. For the purpose of this chapter, we will call these experts the non-amateurs or professionals. We constantly see even the professionals making mistakes. However, over the years they have made more good decisions than bad.

Let's talk for a minute about some of the pitfalls for the amateur investor. One thought all of us may have is, *Where can I make the most money the quickest?* This line of thinking is what gets most of us into trouble. The amateur investor needs to remember there are several areas to consider other than just the rate of return. These all fall under the category of "risk versus reward" and include inflation, production of current income, taxation of the investment, and safety. For your review, we have provided a chart where many investment opportunities are scored on a scale of 1 to 10.

What Are Your Personal Investment Objectives?

In order to understand what you personally want from an investment, you need to decide on several factors. Score yourself below, on the five listed items, from 1 to 10 in each category. A "1" represents that you have little concern about how this factor will affect your investment. A "10" represents that this factor is your greatest concern. Some people are not concerned or affected by taxation, and they want their investments to be very liquid. Others need to consider tax implications, have adequate liquid assets, and want investments that will be protected against the impact of inflation. You decide what your personal objectives are.

	1 to 10
1. INFLATION	_____
2. TAXATION	_____
3. SAFETY	_____
4. LIQUIDITY	_____
5. CURRENT INCOME	_____

Understanding Short-Term Investments

Short-term investment planning means positioning yourself where you can get higher-than-bank interest rates but still have easy access to the money. A short-term investment is a three- to seven-year investment plan. We should not put our emergency cash in such an investment. These investments are usually put into treasury bills, growth mutual funds, annuities, government securities, and bonds.

Most investors are too impatient, especially when dealing with the stock market and mutual fund purchases. We must ride the tide and roll with the punches in order to let the market run its course. We recommend that the average short-term investor purchase balanced mutual funds in order to maximize the return and minimize the risk. The reason for this recommendation is that mutual funds are managed by expert money managers. In general, these funds have averaged 10 to 15 percent annually over the past fifteen years. Even with an average inflation rate of over 5 percent a year, this certainly gives an investor the opportunity to get ahead of the game. Over the same period, annuities have averaged around 7 percent, and they allow the investors to be conservative and safe. Please keep in mind that annuities are sold by insurance companies, so make sure you buy from a quality company.

Understanding Long-Term Investments

Long-term investments are investments of a minimum of seven years, all the way to retirement. These investments should be aggressive for younger people and moderately aggressive for older people. These investments can include stocks, bonds, mutual funds, gold, silver, and antique collections.

One of the main objectives of long-term investments is to ensure plenty of diversification and the investments are not involved for short-range cash needs. For the average investor, it is best to purchase mutual funds comprised of the investments previously mentioned.

One of the crucial mistakes many investors make is constantly playing a guessing game with their investment portfolio. By doing this, most will lose out on the opportunity to be at the right place at the right time.

The financial villains most of us need to worry about are the bankers, the insurance salesmen, and the stockbrokers who constantly try to move us from one investment to another in order to get us the newest, hottest deal. Another financial villain is the hidden villain called *inflation*. Inflation has averaged over 6 percent the past fifteen years.

Our common sense tells us that if we put all of our long-term investment into a CD we could be in real trouble. Here's an example:

A bank CD has paid an average of 5 percent during a one-year time frame.

Table of Net Earnings on a Five Percent CD

Investment of $1,000	Interest of 5%	**Earnings of**	**$50.00**
Taxes on Earnings	Rate of 20%	**Less Taxes of**	**$10.00**
Total Investment, Plus Earnings, Less Taxes			**$1040.00**
Less Annual Inflation	Inflation Rate of 6% Equals <$60.00>	**Leaves You a Balance of**	**$980.00**
Your Total Net Earnings			**<$20.00>**

That is not a pretty picture. Your 5 percent earnings do not really keep up with inflation. Mutual funds have averaged 15 percent over the same time frame, which would at least keep you out of a negative situation. The real issue is that most of us are amateurs when it comes to long-term planning. And we have experts handling mutual funds in order to maximize our investment dollars.

Analysis of Different Investments

Pick the investments that you currently have, or have been thinking about, and see how they score in each category that is important to you. The following scores are based on a scale of 1 to 10 and measure tax treatment, inflation, liquidity, income, and safety. A score of 1 represents the least desirable, and 10 represents the most desirable. (Example: A universal or adjustable life insurance policy scores as follows: 8 in taxation, because its cash values accrue tax deferred until withdrawn; 9 in liquidity, because its cash value is liquid at any time; 8 in inflation, because death benefits have the opportunity to increase; 6 in income, because of its deferred value for retirement; and 9 in safety, because of its reserves and assets of major insurance companies.)

Investments Table

Investment	Inflation	Taxation	Safety	Liquidity	Income
Business Interest	8	9	4	3	8
Real Estate	8	8	5	4	4
Growth Mutual Funds	9	6	5	9	3
Real Estate Partnership	8	7	5	4	6
Apartments	8	7	5	4	5
Commercial Real Estate	8	7	5	4	5
Personal Residence	8	7	5	4	5
Rental Home	8	7	5	4	5
Common Stock	9	5	5	9	5
Public Utility Stock Funds	7	6	8	9	8

Investment	Inflation	Taxation	Safety	Liquidity	Income
Oil and Gas Drilling Program	8	7	3	3	3
Growth and Current Income Fund	8	5	6	9	5
Balanced Mutual Funds	8	5	6	9	6
Participating Mutual Funds	7	5	8	4	8
Gold and Silver	7	6	6	6	2
Real Estate Investment Trust	7	6	5	8	8
Diamonds and Gemstones	7	6	5	4	2
Specialized Mutual Funds	8	5	4	9	4
Income Mutual Funds	7	5	7	9	8
Collectibles	7	6	4	4	2
Oil and Gas Balances Programs	7	6	4	3	5
Life Insurance (Universal of Adjustable Life)	8	7	9	9	6
Commodities	7	6	4	4	2
Agriculture and Ranching	7	5	5	4	5
Real Estate Partnerships	6	5	7	4	7
Vacation Home	7	5	4	5	2
Undeveloped Land	8	3	4	4	2
Oil and Gas Income Program	6	5	4	4	7
Preferred Stocks	5	5	7	9	7
Tax Exempt Bond Funds	2	8	9	9	6
Tax Free Unit Trust	2	8	9	9	9

Investment	Inflation	Taxation	Safety	Liquidity	Income
GNMA and FNMA Trust	4	3	9	9	9
Equipment Leasing Program	3	6	5	3	8
Treasury Bonds	2	5	10	10	7
Corporate Bonds	3	4	7	9	8
Zero Coupon Bonds	2	3	9	9	2
U.S. Government Security Mutual Funds	2	3	9	9	8
Savings Accounts and CDs	2	2	10	10	6
Money Market Funds	2	2	10	10	7

The preceding table compares various asset types with five financial concerns. These assets are not based on any information about your specific needs or financial circumstances. The amateur investor needs to consider short-term and long-term investment strategies. For the amateur investor, choosing such investments as oil and gas leases, shopping centers, futures, etc., is not ideal from a risk standpoint. The following sections provide an understanding of the most common short- and long-term investments.

Understanding Mutual Funds

A mutual fund is a type of investment that has the following characteristics:

1. There is diversification of an investment dollar into various investments, without direct ownership of stock, bonds, government papers,

    etc., and without the direct risk of such invest-
ments.
2. Money in a mutual fund is managed by
professional money managers.
3. Funds have charges for professional management.
   A. Front-end load
   B. Back-end load
   C. Middle load
4. The purpose of a fund is to diversify ownership
and risk, but still reap a potentially high rate
of return.

Types of Mutual Funds

1. Stock Mutual Funds
   - Growth stock.
   - Aggressive growth stock.
   - Balanced fund made up of bonds and stocks.
   - Pool ownership of stocks.
2. Bond Mutual Funds
   - Corporate bond fund, made up of various corporate bonds.
   - Municipal bond fund, composed of many municipalities bonds paying tax exempt earnings.
   - Some corporate bond funds are tax exempt as well.
   - Bonds are loans to corporations, and you are participating in the diversification of many companies.
3. Government Securities Funds
   - GNMA government loans.
   - T-bills.
   - Government bonds and various other government papers.
4. International or World Funds
   - Ownership of stock in various economies.
   - More risky, but more potential earnings.

- Purpose is to invest in major corporations of many countries.
5. Precious Metals Funds
   - Gold.
   - Silver.
   - Various other precious metals.
   - Purpose is to diversify ownership into different metals.

With short-term investing, it is important to know if and when there are any penalties for withdrawing your money. Most annuities have a penalty up front of about 7 percent if you get out early. Most mutual funds have a 5 to 8 percent load, up front. The short-term investor should be leery if someone says there are no charges in moving in and out of an investment.

Understanding Mutual Funds

Most investors will be safer dealing with mutual funds. Mutual funds are a group of investments pooled together and managed by professional money managers. There are various types of mutual funds, and they can be used as long-term and short-term investments. Mutual funds keep the amateur investor from having to make choices on stocks, bonds, money markets, or government securities, by placing all of these risks in various mutual funds. As in stock, the mutual funds are sold in shares; therefore, people throughout the country are mutually investing in the funds along with you.

We must be careful about the loading charges on mutual funds. There are three ways to charge the customer for the purchase of a mutual fund: Front-end, back-end, or middle-loaded. Front-end loaded mutual funds are ideal, but the cost should run 5 percent or less of the initial investment. The reason this is ideal is that you pay no charge to get out of the fund on the backside. You pay only 5 percent maximum on the money put into the fund. The 5 percent can decrease as you put larger sums into the fund.

Many people ask about "no load" funds. There *are* funds called no load. But remember, there is no free lunch! A no load fund either takes a percentage each year called a management fee or administrative fee, or they take it on the back-end when you sell out of the fund. If this is done, you are paying a percentage on the total growth of your principal over a period of time.

Over the past fifteen years, mutual funds have averaged between 12 to 15 percent per year return. Obviously, some have performed at a lesser rate and some at a higher rate. This type of an investment is versatile and safe. This gives the investor the opportunity to do well and minimize the risk, while the professionals do the work. Mutual funds should be used as an investment of at least two to three years and can easily serve as a five- to fifteen-year investment tool.

Many people become impatient with mutual funds and want instant gratification. They see the stock market fall 300 points and want to sell off and run for the hills. *Do not do this!* Funds will average themselves over a period of time. Consistency and persistency are the keys to being successful in funds.

Average Annual Investment Returns, from 1926 to 1991

1. Bank Certificates of Deposit (CDs)
3.5% per year

2. Insurance Company Annuities
4.5% per year

3. Dow Jones Stock Index
(top 50 companies)
7.0% per year

Understanding Annuities

Annuities are the insurance company's answer to CDs offered by the banks.

- They guarantee an interest rate of about 4.5 percent per year.
- They are guaranteed by the assets of the insurance company.
- They can be used as an investment, or they can be used as a form of payment distribution on a monthly basis.
- Since 1926, they have averaged approximately 4.5 percent per year.
- The past ten years the rates have averaged between 7 and 8 1/2 percent per year.

What Types Of Annuities Are Available?

1. Single Premium Tax Deferred
   - All earnings are tax deferred until withdrawn.
   - Money is placed in a lump sum into an annuity.
   - Tax is paid when money is pulled out of the annuity.
   - Money that is put into this annuity is taxable before it is invested.
2. Tax Deferred Annuity
   - Money is put in periodically, instead of in a lump sum.
   - Tax is paid when money is withdrawn.
   - Tax is paid on the original investment before invested.

- Early surrender charges apply for approximately seven to ten years.
3. Flexible Annuity
   - Money is taxable before being invested.
   - You can vary deposits anytime.
   - Earnings are taxable as they accrue.
   - Interest rates fluctuate annually or, in some cases, monthly.
   - Can be used as a retirement vehicle on short-term investments.
   - Early withdrawal penalties apply for up to ten years into the contract, usually five to seven years.
4. Variable Annuities
   - Similar to variable life, except there is no death benefit other than the value of the annuity.
   - Individual investors are allowed investment choices.
   - Choices are related to mutual fund or stock market.
   - Has highest potential earnings but also the most risk.
   - Early withdrawal penalties apply for five to ten years, depending on investment company.

Single Premium Tax-Deferred Annuity

Let's look at another safe investment for the amateur—annuities. There are various types of annuities, but the most common type, referred to as a long-term investment, is the *single premium tax deferred annuity.* This is where the investor puts a sum of money into an insurance company's annuity at a set interest rate for one year at a time. Every twelve months the rates change. The nice thing about this investment is the earnings are tax deferred until you pull them out. These investments typically make one to two percent a year—more than a bank's

CD. However, CDs are not tax deferred, so this makes annuity investments very attractive in comparison. As a side note, CDs have averaged 3.5 percent per year over the last sixty-seven years. And annuities have averaged 4.5 percent per year during the same time frame.

There is another important point that must be made about investing in mutual funds and annuities. A cost-averaging method should be used. This means that each month, or once every three months, money should be placed into the investment of your choice. It should be done *consistently*. Cost averaging will enable you to maximize buying opportunities on funds and annuities if you do it regularly, because the average rate will produce positive investment return.

Before we leave annuities, let's look at their loading charges. A good annuity should have no more than a 7 percent withdrawal penalty. After owning the annuity for seven years, there should be no penalty for withdrawal. Here's how it works: Each year the withdrawal percentage should drop about 1 percent until, after seven years, there is no charge at all. Many annuities are being sold that have as much as a 20 percent loading fee, for up to fifteen years.

The following is an example of the effect a loading fee can have on earnings if you withdraw your money prematurely:

Loading cost	7%
Investment amount	$1,000
Term of investment	1 year
Rate of return	7%
Your earnings	0%

After one year, your earnings of 7 percent are washed out by the loading cost of 7 percent. So, in effect, you have earned no money. Ask questions, and be aware of what you are doing when you're investing.

Understanding Certificates of Deposit

Another facet of short-term investing is a bank certificate of deposit (CD), or high-yield money market fund. These CD accounts have no risk up to $100,000, allowing you to accumulate minimum earnings. However, we must be careful when making CD decisions due to the early withdrawal penalties. The ideal CD should be purchased for no longer than six months to one year.

A great example of a person who has worked well with an investment strategy is Donna. Donna is a thirty-seven-year-old widow. She walked into our office one day, looking for a financial advisor, and stated that her local banker had recommended us for financial counseling. The money that she had to invest came from the proceeds from her husband's death. Her husband, Bill, had died in a plane crash at the young age of thirty-nine. Bill left her $600,000 to invest. Most of our clients do not have such a large sum of money to invest.

After several meetings, we agreed that she could live on $36,000 per year. Therefore, we wanted to establish a financial game plan that would produce this income plus any surplus earnings. We chose eight different mutual funds for diversification and three, six-month CDs. This was approximately eight years ago; today, Donna has more than her original $600,000 and has lived a comfortable lifestyle for the last eight years.

Short- and Long-term Investments Are for the Average American

Many people think that only those with large estates and large annual incomes need to do financial planning. But most of our clients are average-income Americans, just hard-working folks.

Let's talk about Robert and Shannon. They are a thirty-two-year-old married couple. Robert is an electrician making $28,000 per year for the local school district. Robert and Shannon have two children, ages eight and twelve. They live in a modest home and drive a pickup truck and station wagon. They started the planning process ten years ago and, we are proud to say, are doing well.

The first financial move they made was to purchase a $50,000 life insurance policy that paid dividends. This policy was adjustable—annually, as needs and income have risen, they have been able to adjust the coverage needed. They had a new will drawn up, which they have recently revised. They put $50 a month into a mutual fund and have a $5,000 emergency fund account set aside. Also, they are faithful to their budget.

Personal Investment Planning

Each person's financial diversification should be individually designed, but the number on the following chart is a generalization of a safe, well-balanced mix of investments. Analyze the investments on your financial statement to determine if your investment strategy is properly balanced. Divide your investment categories by your net worth to determine your percentage.

RISK AND REWARD		INVESTMENT	EQUITY	
		1. Amount of Asset	Totals %	Ideal %
Very Low	Cash and Checking Accounts	$		
	T-Bills, Govt. Bonds & Money Market	$		
	Savings Accounts & CDs	$		
	Total Very Low Risk		%	10%
Low	Municipal Bonds/Funds	$		
	Corporate Bonds/Income Mutual Funds	$		
	Notes & Mortgages Receivables	$		
	Life Insurance Cash Value	$		
	Fixed Annuities	$		
	Total Low Risk		%	20%
Medium	IRA, Keogh, TSA, 401K Plans	$		
	Corporate Qualified Plans (vested)	$		
	Residence (Home)	$		
	Common or Preferred Stock	$		
	Capital Accumulation Mutual Funds	$		
	Growth Mutual Funds	$		
	Variable Annuities	$		
	Income Real Property			
	Total Medium Risk		%	50%
High	Undeveloped Land Real Estate Partnerships			

Energy Exploration
Partnerships

Equipment Lease,
R & D, and
Tax Shelters   _____

Business Interest

Agriculture and
Ranching   _____

Art, Antiques,
Stamps, and Gems_____

Gold, Silver, and
Coins   _____

Total High Risk _____% _____18%

Very
High

Commodities/
Options   _____

Personal property/
Bequests

Automobiles   _____

Recreational
Property   _____

Other Loans &
Liabilities   _____

(credit cards)   _____

Total Very High Risk _____% _____2%

CHAPTER FOURTEEN

Life Insurance Is a Matter of Life and Death

After twenty years of discussing life insurance with many clients, it is apparent that this is a confusing issue for most people. It's also a subject almost everyone has an opinion about. Probably 80 to 85 percent of us do not understand as much as we should to make wise decisions about life insurance.

Life insurance companies are in the business of making a profit. They enjoy selling us the less expensive term insurance most people lean toward; this is because most people outlive the policies, making it profitable for the companies. If they sell the expensive whole life products, they get their money up front and pay you a low return on the backside. That means if you drop the policies after having them for a few years, you lose out all the way around. So you can see it is important to educate ourselves about insurance, so that the decisions we make will be the right ones.

Always buy the kind of life insurance that will be in force the day you die.

It truly is a matter of life and death, financially speaking, for the survivors of many families in our country. Many heads of households who bring home the bacon, whether they be male or female, feel that whatever life insurance coverage their employer offers is all they need. If we have heard this once, we have heard it a thousand times. Here's an example of a typical American family.

Jerry and Beth were a happy couple, with two teenagers and one nine-year-old daughter. Jerry made approximately $40,000 annually, and Beth stayed at home with the children. Jerry was in perfect health, until one day during an annual physical they found a lump or mass in his colon. Within three months, Jerry died. Beth came into our office, and we reviewed Jerry's insurance policy proceeds that Beth would receive. She was going to get $108,000 from his company plan.

When Beth asked what her monthly income would be, our reply was "$850 per month, if we're lucky." She could not believe the words. Here's how it works:

$108,000.00 (investment money) at 10% (return) = $10,800.00
$10,800.00 divided by 12 months = $850.00 per month

This scenario is relived time and time again in our society. If Jerry had had $400,000 to $500,000 worth of life insurance, it would have produced $40,000 to $50,000 dollars of income for his family to maintain their standard of living. We are sure some of you, as you read this formula, may say that with Jerry's death, the monthly amount needed to support the family would decrease. This may be somewhat true. But even if dropped 20 to 25 percent per month, there will be taxes of 20 to 25 percent for Beth to pay out of her earnings.

Some Important Facts about Insurance

It is important to understand that life insurance dollars can be bought for one to two cents on the dollar. How much it will actually cost you depends on your age and health risk factors. If your health has been good, you do not smoke or abuse your body with drugs and alcohol, and you have a good genetic history, your insurance costs will be less than if you have any risk factors. Take care of yourself physically and it will help when you need to get insurance. We know several people who are essentially uninsurable because of excessive weight, smoking, alcohol abuse, and the like.

Insurance dollars are paid to the beneficiary in such a way as to protect your estate. When they are paid out in a lump sum to the beneficiary, they are paid federal income tax free.

Most people should own no less than 50 percent of their insurance coverage personally. If your health changes it may be hard to get insurance. If you leave your job and you have had some health problems, the group insurance you had at the job may no longer be available to you. Your coverage may be totally lost. Many mistakenly think that having plenty of group life insurance is their security blanket and all the insurance they need.

Also, in today's world, life insurance can act as a good short-term or long-term investment because of the universal and adjustable life policies that accrue a cash value on a tax-deferred basis. Most of these policies pay 6 to 7 percent annual return, which will usually out perform a bank CD.

How Much Insurance Do You Need?

A good rule of thumb concerning how much insurance a person needs to maintain the family's current lifestyle *is a minimum of eight times your annual earnings, minus your liquid assets,* regardless of what kind of coverage you buy. This is based on the assumption that a wise investment program will yield 10 percent per year. In the current atmosphere of deflated interest earnings, you might only realize a 7 percent earnings without risking principle. In this case, you may need insurance equal to ten times your annual earnings to provide for your family and uphold their same lifestyle.

One of the most serious problems a spouse makes in life's financial journey is not taking care of the surviving family members in the event of his or her death. When interviewed, some spouses will say, "When I'm dead and gone they will have to do the best they can." This is a response that probably does not reflect their true desires, but reflects their denial about facing their own mortality. Most of us want to continue to protect and support our family even after we are gone, but we really do not want to think about being gone. Life insurance, if used properly in one's financial planning, can protect the estate that we have spent years developing. And it can help ensure our family's financial wellness.

In dealing with the steps to financial wellness, life insurance is probably one of the single weakest links in the financial programs reviewed by the authors of this book. Life insurance is given the least attention by many and causes the most financial devastation for family members who are left behind.

What Kind of Insurance Do You Need?

"Always buy the kind of life insurance that will be in force the day that you die." You heard us say that before. There is also the age-old question of whether life insurance is a bad investment, and whether we should all buy term insurance and invest the difference.

The truth is that not all life insurance is a bad investment, but some life insurance companies' products may be bad investments. Therefore, we must be aware of the person and company who sells us our life insurance. There are over 2,500 life insurance companies out of which only 75 to 100 are top notch. Let's look at some different types of companies and policies that are being sold.

Term Life Insurance

As we get older, this type of insurance goes up in price, or the coverage decreases as inflation increases. It's OK to own term insurance, but we would *not suggest* that more than *50 percent* of your total coverage be in term insurance. Term insurance should be used in short-term need situations, not long-term, due to its coverage expiring before you die and its higher cost that will come in later years. We must remember that term insurance is a form of coverage to indemnify us for a short term. The very nature of the word *term* tells us that this coverage is restricted to a short-term period. In later years, most people end up dropping the coverage, and the insurance *companies love them for it*. The reason most people will drop this coverage in later years is due to the heavily escalating premiums. If you are sure that you will die by age seventy and you have a lot of money for premiums, then term insurance could be considered a decent buy.

Whole Life Insurance

This type of insurance has encountered much negative press over the years. This type of policy accrues money just like a savings account. The savings is called *guaranteed cash value,* which is a return of your premium and the interest you have earned. For lack of a better term, we will call this an escrow account as the money builds up. A whole life policy can also accrue an annual dividend if you are with a mutual insurance company. If you are not with a mutual insurance company, then you have probably bought a nondividend policy from a stock company. As we mentioned in chapter 7, a policy that pays dividends is called a *participating policy,* issued by a mutual company. A stock company's policy typically pays no dividends and, therefore, is called *nonparticipating.* (We will go into more detail about different types of companies later.)

With a whole life insurance policy, the premium stays level, and so does the death benefit. In most cases, the worst thing that this policy will do is give you your premiums back, if you live to the retirement age of sixty-five or older.

Universal Life Insurance

This policy is interest- and mortality-sensitive. In other words, you pay your premiums for a set amount of death benefit. However, your premium is subject to change later if the interest rate that the insurance company is initially paying, and says they are going to pay for the future, does not become a reality. Then, the premium must be increased to keep the coverage from expiring. For example, an insurance company may propose a large death benefit with a small premium and use a future earnings rate assumption of 11 percent, when the current rates are 6 to 6-1/2 percent. It is reasonable to assume that this is an exaggerated projection that could lead to a terminated insurance policy or higher premiums to the policyholder later on.

Adjustable Life Insurance

This type of policy is recognized for its flexibility. The policy premium and face amount can be adjusted as needed by the policyholder. This policy is used more today than ever before because it can be custom designed and does not depend on just interest-rate performance for its cash accrual. This policy is also more dividend-sensitive annually, which means that the premiums, coverage, and length of coverage are contingent upon the amount of annual dividends by the insurance company to the insured. In this plan, dividends paid annually to the policyholder can be used to extend the coverage period, keep the premiums low, and keep the coverage constant. This plan also accrues cash value due to the dividends, similar to universal life and whole life. Adjustable life has one feature that is unique to life insurance policies—a cost-of-living index. This index increases the coverage periodically to keep the policy in pace with inflation. When purchasing adjustable life insurance it is important to make sure that the policy pays a dividend and has a cost-of-living index.

Single Premium Life Insurance

This type of life insurance is used when an investor makes a one-time deposit into the policy. This premium will either draw a current interest rate and/or annual dividends.

The dividends or interest will accrue tax deferred until the policyholder pulls the money out. Most insurance companies will allow you, under current tax laws, to pull the earnings out annually, without tax. They can do this by calling it a loan and paying a crediting rate equal to your loan rate.

This means you can get an interest-free loan through tax-deferred earnings. This is an excellent way to get tax-deferred earnings at higher than most institutions' interest rates, without the penalties related to IRAs and annuities.

The single premium life insurance plan is an excellent consideration for money that presently goes to IRAs where the investor has lost the IRA deduction due to involvement in a qualified retirement plan.

Variable Life Insurance

This type of life insurance is the newest kid on the block. This insurance allows the customer to choose the way annual premiums will be invested by the insurance company. The investment choices can include money market, common stock, bonds, and annuities. The average life insurance investor needs to be careful that he gets good financial advice on this policy.

Be Honest About What You Value

In the late 1970s, an insurance review was done on a couple named Doug and Dorothy. Doug was a take-charge sales executive who had definite ideas about his insurance planning process. He believed strongly in the importance of life insurance, but only for himself as the head of the household. His attitude was that his wife did not work so there was no need for coverage other than what his company provided for her. They had two children, ages five and eleven. We continually counseled him to think about child care costs should anything happen to his wife. However, Doug would not budge on the subject. Sadly, two days after our last annual review of the family insurance program, Dorothy was shot and killed by an intruder in their home.

Doug was emotionally devastated, and the amount of coverage on Dorothy was only $5,000. In making the funeral arrangements, the cost came to $9,000, leaving a $4,000 shortage. But all the debts were the real financial problem, plus the ensuing child care expenses.

Do You Own the Correct Amount of Life Insurance?

Yes/No

1. Is your insurance adequate to pay off your mortgage? (if applicable) _____

2. Is your insurance sufficient to pay off all final expenses and burial (approximately $10,000)?

   _____

3. Does your insurance provide for education of your children in the event of premature death? (if applicable) _____

4. What percentage of your life insurance is group insurance?
If exceeds 33%	0 points
16% to 33%	10 points
Less than 16%	20 points	_____

5. What percentage of your insurance is term insurance?

If exceeds 50%	0 points
25% to 50%	10 points
Less than 25%	20 points _____

Scoring: Each yes (answers to questions 1-3) is worth 20 points. Add these points to the points scored on questions 4-5 to get the sum.

1. _____
2. _____
3. _____
4. _____
5. _____
_____ **TOTAL**

Evaluation: Points

Excellent	100
Very good	90
Good	80
Fair	70
Poor	60
Very poor	50

For illustrations of a life insurance policy, see Appendix C.

CHAPTER FIFTEEN

Retirement Planning

As stated in the **TOTAL PERSON** part of this book, retirement can be whenever you want it to be; it depends on how smart you are in your short-term and long-term investment strategies. Most people in our country feel that retirement is something "I'll worry about when I get older" or that "the Social Security system will take care of me." Wrong! Retirement is our own personal responsibility, and no one else is going to worry about it. Following are some tips that may help.

1. *Get an IRA*—preferably not a CD, but a well-balanced mutual fund.
2. *Join the retirement plan* at your company; put in at least 4 to 5 percent of your pay every pay period.
3. *Don't count on Social Security.*
4. *Set up a KEOUGH,* or a SEP if you are self-employed.

Remember that retirement is not a *figment* of our imagination and something that just happens to the old man down the street. It's real, and it's going to happen to us all if we live long enough.

You must remember that approximately 90 percent of those who live to retirement age end up on Social Security as the main source of income. This is a terrible thought for most young people who are living on $2,000 to $4,000 a month. In the future they are going to live on $1,000 a month.

In order to make retirement work, we must do the other eight steps first. Too many people have an IRA account or put 15 percent of their pay into the company retirement plan and still don't have the money to fix the car or buy a new washer without charging it. Don't procrastinate about retirement. Start planning your retirement *today* as part of your total financial wellness program.

401K Planning Decisions for Retirement

1. Stock Funds

Typically consists of growth or aggressive growth stocks with double digit earning potential.

2. Guaranteed Interest Accounts

Usually are annuities with 7 to 9 percent per year earning potential.

3. Bond Funds

Usually corporate bonds with 6 to 8 percent yearly potential.

4. Real Estate

Normally consists of real estate ownership in shopping centers, high rises, and apartment buildings.

5. Money Markets

Usually consists of government papers with little risk and low earning potential.

6. International Funds

Consist of ownership of several major nations' corporate stock (for example, Japan, France, Great Britain, Italy). Be careful though because this involves higher potential earnings with more potential risk.

As we have said, retirement does not just happen. It is a privilege that must be taken seriously and planned, just like the weekly family schedule of events.

— • • • —

Don't Start to Begin to Get Ready Tomorrow. Do It Today

— • • • —

CHAPTER SIXTEEN

Where There's a Will There's an Easier Way

Most people do not have a will because they believe that they do not own enough possessions to justify it. Approximately eight out of ten people who come to us for consultation do not have a will. However, even if you are single and have few possessions or debts, you still do not want your family to be left paying off your credit cards or the government owning your personal belongings.

In most states, if you are married, only one-half of your possessions will automatically go to the spouse if you die. The remainder will go to the courts to decide what the disposition will be. If you have children, the courts even get to decide who will raise your children. When we die without a will, the children's future sometimes falls into the hands of a judge whom you have never met.

The irony is that most people do not want to deal with a lawyer or *spend the money*. But the truth is, if you die without a will, you'll pay more in legal fees and have little control over the financial destiny of your estate. There are several types of wills.

Holographic Wills

The first type of will is *holographic*. This is when you fill out your own will on a blank piece of paper at home and state that, in the event of your death, you leave everything to your spouse. The disadvantage is that you may not conform to all the state laws; in many cases the will is not properly witnessed or notarized to make it legally binding. This may make it easy for someone to contest it. Then, your will may not be followed.

Bookstore Wills

Another type of will is a *bookstore will*. You can get a preprinted form at your friendly stationery store or answer a television ad for a preprinted will. Just fill in the blanks. However, most bookstore wills may not give you enough options to fully distribute your estate to the various parties. Also they may not legally protect you from a variety of unforeseen disputes. Just as with the holographic will, the lack of having witnesses and the uncertainty that you are complying with state laws may also make the bookstore wills inadequate.

Last Will and Testament

BE IT KNOWN, that I, _____, a resident of _____, being of sound mind, do make and declare this to be my Last Will and Testament, expressly revoking all my prior Wills and Codicils at any time made.

I. PERSONAL REPRESENTATION:
    I appoint _____, of _____, as Personal Representative of this my Last Will and Tes-

tament and provide if this Personal Representative is unable or unwilling to serve then I appoint _____ _____, as alternative Personal Representative. My Personal Representative shall be authorized to carry out all provisions of this Will and pay my just debts, obligations, and funeral expenses. I further provide my Personal Representative shall not be required to post surety bond in this or any other jurisdiction, and direct that no expert appraisal be made of my estate unless required by law.

II. GUARDIAN:

In the event I shall die as the sole parent of minor children, then I appoint _____, as Guardian of said minor children. If this named Guardian is unable or unwilling to serve, then I appoint _____ _____ as alternate Guardian.

III. BEQUESTS:

I direct that after payment of all my just debts, my property be bequeathed in the manner following:

IN WITNESS WHEREOF, I have hereunto set my hand this _____ day of _____, 19___, to this my Last Will and Testament.

_____
Signature

IV. WITNESSED:

This Last Will and Testament of _____
was signed and declared to be his/her Last Will and
Testament in our presence and his/her request and in the
presence of each other, we do hereby witness same on this
_____day of _____, 19___.

_____   _____

_____   _____

_____   _____

Witness Signature (3)   Address

Legal Document Store Wills

The third type of will is the *Legal Document Store* variety
where a law firm sells you a boilerplate will and fills in a
few specifics about you and your desires. In our recent
research, we have found that you can buy a will for as
little as $75 from certain discount law firms. This is still a
fill-in-the-blank type of instrument, and it may be sufficient for some single people with simple estates. However, the more complicated your estate and family, the
more likely something important will be missed without
getting good legal counsel, estate planning, and will
preparation. Even though this boilerplate will is better
than nothing, our advice is to spend a few more dollars
and have a custom will made to meet your specific needs.

The Custom-Made Estate Wills

This will can cost from $100 to $500. By going this route,
you can address several issues, take an inventory of all
your possessions, and list in the will your specific distribution to family members. You can deal with long-range
goals, name a trustee for your children's money, and
name a guardian for your children. When doing a custo-

mized will, you can add a power of attorney. You can also create a "living will," which addresses such issues as directions to physicians about life support machines.

If you are going to follow all of our other steps toward financial health and building a healthy estate, then don't you want to be the one to decide where it all goes when you die? You can only do this with a will. If you have no instrument to address your assets distribution, then you ensure that lawyers will get a bigger piece of your estate while the family fights in court over money or child custody.

Where There's a Will There's an Easier Way

Joe was a forty-eight-year-old, hardworking oil man— the gruff, teddy-bear type, with coal-black hair tinged with gray. Many times we had talked about wills and life insurance to plan his estate. Joe would constantly tell us that he was "insurance poor" and didn't want some lawyer telling him how to run his business. One cold December evening Joe was traveling home and was killed in a head-on collision with a drunk driver.

Unfortunately, Joe was only insured for $100,000, and his family was used to his making $60,000 a year. As you might have already guessed, Joe died without a will of any kind. Joe had a nice income but a lot of debt. His wife, Mary, and their two children were used to living on $5,000 a month. But no more. Because Joe had no will, it took fourteen months of legal and family squabbles about many issues, including ownership of rental properties, to settle Joe's business affairs. The legal bills ran up to approximately $15,000 before Mary got legal resolution.

One of her brothers-in-law claimed Joe had promised him one of his rental houses because he had helped Joe paint and fix it up. However, Joe had never told Mary about this, so uncertainty and disagreement drove a wedge between the relationships in Joe's family. Instead of the $500 for a custom will and $1,000 to probate the will, Mary ended up spending an extra $13,500 because of Joe's desire to save money.

The Bigger Your Estate, the Bigger Your Tax Bill

When you die, the government will tax your estate. If you have practiced a prudent financial wellness program and built a sizeable estate, then the taxes could also be sizeable. Look at the chart below to understand how taxes can impact an estate.

What It Costs to Die Rich

Size of Estate at Death	Tax Due on Estate
$750,000	**$248,300**
$1,000,000	**$345,800**
$1,500,000	**$555,800**
$2,000,000	**$780,000**
$2,500,000	**$1,025,800**
$3,000,000	**$1,290,000**
$5,000,000	**$2,390,000**
$7,500,000	**$3,765,800**
$10,000,000	**$5,140,000**
$15,000,000	**$7,890,800**
$20,000,000	**$10,640,800**

Where the Cash Comes from to Pay Your Estate Taxes

Unless you qualify for special payment arrangements, your taxes must be paid in cash within nine months after the date of your death. Depending on how you answer the following questions, you may leave your family in a difficult financial situation.

1. Is life insurance a good vehicle for tax payment? (yes/no)
2. Is a properly designed will and trust a good vehicle to save estate tax? (yes/no)

The answer to both questions is yes.

The Impact of Estate Taxes and Settlement Fees on Those Who Have Died with Money

Famous Person	Gross Estate	Total Settlement Cost	Net Estate	Percent Shrinkage
Marilyn Monroe	$819,176	$448,750	$370,426	55%
W. C. Fields	$884,680	$329,793	$554,887	37%
Humphrey Bogart	$910,146	$274,234	$635,912	30%
Franklin D. Roosevelt	$1,940,999	$574,867	$1,366,132	30%
Clark Gable	$2,806,526	$1,101,308	$1,705,488	30%
Gary Cooper	$4,984,985	$1,530,454	$3,454,531	31%
Elvis Presley	$10,165,434	$7,374,635	$2,790,799	73%

Famous Person	Gross Estate	Total Settlement Cost	Net Estate	Percent Shrinkage
John D. Rockefeller, Sr.	$26,905,182	$17,124,988	$9,780,194	64%
Walt Disney	$23,004,851	$6,811,943	$16,192,908	30%
Dean Witter	$7,451,055	$1,830,717	$5,620,338	25%
Alvin C. Ernst, CPA	$12,642,431	$7,124,112	$5,518,319	56%
Howard Gould	$67,635,386	$52,549,682	$14,985,704	78%

Create When You Are Young, Preserve When You Are Older

In reviewing the above chart you may have noticed that even wealthy people need a financial plan. For example, Elvis Presley's estate was reduced by 73 percent due to lack of planning. Many people feel that only the young or poor need insurance. Other people argue that if you have plenty of money, insurance and wills are not necessary. The truth is that everyone needs some insurance, a will, estate planning, etc. When you are young you need to produce assets and protect your family in case of a premature death. When you are older, with a sizable estate, you need to protect your family from taxes and distribute the estate to your heirs. Remember, when you are young, *create* with insurance and wills. When you are older, *preserve and protect* with insurance and wills.

• • •

SECTION IV

Putting It All Together

CHAPTER SEVENTEEN

Putting Your Mind and Spirit Over Money

Money Is the Number One Family Stressor

Many of us *spend* our lives letting money dominate our behavior. In surveys about family stress, money is the number one stressor for both husbands and wives. This book has been an attempt to give you some guidelines to help minimize the stress that money can cause in your life. Whether you make a small or large salary, you can experience financial wellness or financial dysfunction. We know people who make little, yet have much. We know others who have made a fortune yet have little sense of financial security.

Some people who grow up without money often live in fear that they will not make enough money in their adulthood. They may try to hold on to every penny, obsessively. On the other hand, the folks that grew up with plenty of money may not feel an urgency about money and do not, therefore, put realistic value on the dollar. The truth is that despite our financial family of origin, we should be prudent with our money. We should make sure it remains a vehicle to get us through our life's journey, not an obsession.

As we discussed in previous chapters, money can become the focus of our lives. We certainly live in a system that is structured to create future indebtedness. It is important to remember this rule of thumb: If you can't pay cash, or at least pay a debt within ninety days, you should not make the purchase.

Over the years, we have seen relationships ruined over money. Families have been torn apart and creditability turned upside down. Yet the things that are really important in life have no dollar value attached.

Many of us feel overwhelmed with our monthly debt—not just fixed debts but also variable debts. After paying our first of the month bills we start projecting catastrophe about the next few week's debt, thus fueling a host of negative thoughts instead of taking each day as it comes, working on financial issues as they occur. We may constantly have "too much month at the end of the money," but fail to pinpoint our financial focus and prioritize our plans.

Financial Illness Versus Financial Wellness

Financial illness strikes over 90 percent of all Americans. Government statistics tell us that over 90 out of 100 Americans are financial failures by the time they retire at age sixty-five. Personal finance is not something that most people want to discuss when the subject comes up in conversations around the kitchen table. Many people are sick when it comes to dealing with money; it's not recognized by most, though, because spending money is not *illegal* or *immoral*.

There are many reasons for financial failure. It often starts with our parents, who learned from their parents. Poor financial management is handed down through generations. We have talked about addictions and how financial abuse is another form of addiction. Many people have chosen financial abuse as their relief system—their drug of choice—in an attempt to feel better and improve their self-esteem. Purchases of toys, homes, boats, fancy cars, and resort properties are used to buy happiness.

Poor self-esteem forces the financially addictive personality to continue on the treadmill of earning more and more money to feed the addiction. This causes the common symptom known as *workaholism*, which can lead to destructive personal and family strife.

A financial abuse that strikes many people is the abuse of credit cards and, of course, the fantasy getaway sport of "professional shopping." Many people—when lonely, sad, mad, or unhappy—get in the car, head to the mall, and pull out the credit card. This gives them temporary gratification from the reality of day-to-day problems and poor self-image.

When talking to adults and counseling with them on a daily basis, most have one thing in common: They do not have a game plan for the future. Most important of all, they do not know how to achieve their goal, even if they have one.

We have tried to give you a road map and guide to financial wellness. Most of our parents have not done well at dealing with financial issues, often our schools and teachers do not understand these issues, and, therefore, the role models are limited. Hopefully, we have been able to fill in the gaps.

Are You Spending More Than You Make?

Many people are spending more than they make, which means that adding more monthly debt is not solving the problem. You need to be honest with yourself if you are going to go beyond denial and soar into the world of the financially successful. To be financially successful, as it relates to our sense of wholeness as a person, means you feel spiritually and psychologically at peace with yourself . . . and that money is not interfering with your ability to have healthy relationships.

It really doesn't matter how much you make if you make enough to meet your basic food, clothing, and shelter needs. Everything else then becomes relative. A person making $160,000 per year or a person making $16,000 per year can satisfy the basic existence and survival needs.

The person who makes $16,000 per year could have his or her feet on the ground better and be happier with the day-to-day financial situation than the person making many times more. It's a matter of understanding survival needs and how to be happy with a specific income.

Reviewing Your "Wants" Versus Your "Needs"

Sometimes we tell people that their financial problems could be solved if they would define two things—needs versus wants. Needs are not the same as wants, nor will they ever be. We have talked about this earlier in the book, but *please, please, please* consider how important this is for you personally.

Want means, "I want to feel better about myself, and I want people to look up to me and respect me. I want to be somebody. Therefore, I want to purchase something to make me feel better."

Need means that I have certain survival instincts such as food, shelter, clothing, transportation, retirement, and education for children. Everything else falls into the want category. It is OK to buy sports cars, winter homes, 6,000-square-foot offices, boats, and home video cameras. But are we using these possessions to buy our happiness at the expense of financial devastation?

Some people say that they want to be financially responsible and get off the financial merry-go-round. But what must be done to break this cycle?

First, determine why you feel the need to spend your way into oblivion. Money is merely a vehicle to meet our needs. Something drives people to make more and more money, and it is usually a manifestation of their addictive personality. This is where the workaholic tendency develops. It is important to realize that to get off of the financial merry-go-round of more toys equals more happiness, you must discover the underlying dysfunctional beliefs you are avoiding.

Understand What You Really Want from Your Symbols of Success

There are some things we want because we really want them. There are other things we want because we think they will give us what we really want. You may say, "I want a sports car." Ask yourself, "Fine, what do I want from the red sports car?" You may answer, "I want the feeling of adventure (freedom, power) as I drive down the road with the wind in my hair." The sports car is simply the method to get what we truly desire. Unfortunately, we often go through life acquiring objects without knowing what we are trying to experience by having them.

What we really want is the feelings we experience from having our symbols of success. These experiences are contained in words such as *freedom, security, power, happiness, self-worth, success, satisfaction, respect, peace of mind, adventure, and love.*

The possessions we acquire to get these feelings are simply symbols of "the real thing." These symbols include money, job or career, clothes, cars, house, marriage, family, sex, lover, education, degree, and travel. There's absolutely nothing wrong with wanting these symbols. However, it helps to know that they are really a way to get something else, something experiential: security, fun, energy, satisfaction, love, knowledge of God, inner peace.

If you know the experience you are looking for, you can make a list of things that might provide it. Knowing what you really want dramatically improves the chance of finding the methods and behaviors to fulfill it.

Knowing the experiences you seek helps you avoid fear and disappointment. For example, if you know you want adventure and think a red sports car is the way to get it, you also know the sports car is part of a bigger adventure—finding the methods and behaviors that will bring you adventure. If the car does it and you can afford it, fine. If the car doesn't do it or you can't afford it, OK. Next method or behavior, please!

We can fulfill our own desires without material possessions or much outside help. We can give to ourselves right now. Want love? Love yourself. Want joy? Be joyful. Want adventure? The last frontier is the interior of your mind and spirit. Want friends? Be worthy of being befriended.

If we provide ourselves with the experiences we seek, this significantly decreases the frantic pursuit of the symbols of life. "I can't be happy until I get _____." "I can't rest until _____." "My life isn't complete until I _____." There are few desires or intentions we can't fulfill for ourselves, *right now.*

Ironically, once we have given fully to ourselves what we truly need, and have healthy relations and are living our spiritual beliefs, the symbols seem to come naturally. Relationships are an example. Who would you rather be around—a joyful, loving, happy person, or a miserable, needy, unhappy person? Come to know yourself and begin to change yourself into the person you really want to be. Financial wellness will come easier when you're not wasting money on false symbols.

You can use your behaviors and methods to discover your intentions and desires. Of each external thing you want, ask yourself, "What experience am I looking for?" Experiences can be like the layers of an onion. There may be pleasure on the surface, but as you peel back the layers you may find the stinging reality that pleasure is only a *symbol* of contentment, a symbol of peace of mind. When you discover your fundamental desires and intentions, you'll know what you really want.

The Power of Love

We heard a song titled *The Power of Love,* sung by Billy Falcon. The song describes a man in his Mercedes with power steering, seats, and windows. He goes home to his empty house with the swimming pool. His wife is playing tennis, and his son goes to boarding school. The man sits and cries. His symbols have not led to what he truly desires. Billy Falcon says, "He ain't got the power of love." Next, he describes Louis, who drives a beat up old car with "no power nothing," with a big smile on his face while he holds his girlfriend, Grace. His possessions may be few, but "he's got the power of love."

———•·•·•———

Do we value love, and do our behaviors reflect it? Do we tell those important to us that we care, or do we get caught in the pursuit of the petty pot of gold at the end of the plastic rainbow?

———•·•·•———

Live within Your Means

Alvin Tofler wrote a book titled *Future Shock* that talked about mankind reaching the tolerable limits of change. Below, we have taken the liberty to rework one of his quotations to fit the current world in terms of financial wellness.

———•·•·•———

There are discernible limits to the amount of charging that normal credit can absorb. . . . By endlessly accelerating charges without first determining their limits, we may submit our recreational consumerism to demands they simply cannot tolerate.

———•·•·•———

One of the keys to not accelerating your charges is to have a good budget and to know where you stand financially. The word *budget* is one of the keys to avoiding financial devastation. There is no way to control spending, plan education, plan retirement, plan vacation, or even take care of basic needs without budgeting your money. Ask yourself a question: How can I know what my resources are if I don't know where they are coming from? Remember, we would not build a skyscraper or a home without a blueprint or without knowing the estimated cost. Nevertheless, people operate without a written budget.

More than telling you what you are spending, the budget tells you what you cannot spend. This helps you separate wants from needs.

In a total of forty years of working with individuals, small business owners, professional athletes, etc., the authors have found that most people fail in the area of the written budget. Many tell us they are going to save for retirement, but most cannot tell us how much they need to set aside or how long the process should continue. Without a budget, they have few clues to the answers.

Once you have a budget, you realize that the age-old cliché holds true—*It's not how much you make, but what you do with it.*

The Budget for True Happiness

Simple Living: One Couple's Search for a Better Life, by Frank Levering and Wanda Urbanska, is a guide about couples who had "colossal financial success," but felt terribly alone and abandoned. Some of these couples "gave it all away" and found a renewed quality of life in small towns, meaningful humanitarian jobs, and wonderful relationships with the spouses they were ready to divorce. These couples started making investments in the right places. Perhaps there is value in some of the Quaker practices of voluntary simplicity, avoidance of luxury, and minimizing our material desires.

———•••———

Success and security are intangibles. They are not your standard of living, but your standard of life.

———•••———

Real change ... happens gradually, in fits and starts, in an internal tug-of-war between the deep-rooted claims of the old self and the yearnings to reach for something better.

Frank Levering and Wanda Urbanska,
American authors

• • •

In God We Trust, Let All Others Bring Cash

One of the biggest problems facing people is trust in financial advice. Therefore, they will continue to fail daily at financial management. Your local banker wants you to invest in his low-yield CDs, your insurance agent wants you to purchase her firm's latest product, and your investment stockbroker is giving you the most recent hot tip issued by his investment firm. This is all enough to make the most optimistic person a skeptic. Many have spent years making the wrong financial decisions. Therefore, it is important to be patient in your financial planning process. Try to affiliate with those advisors whom you personally know from church or service organizations. Pick people with strong morals and values.

The Model of Financial Wellness

George and Diane have been clients for over eighteen years. George is a fifty-two-year-old who is soft-spoken, kind, and level headed. He owns a motor repair shop in a low-income part of town where hardworking blue-collar work takes place daily. Diane watches over the family money and keeps the company books.

George and Diane are financially in control of their lives and have always been resourceful. When their income increased, they were careful not to increase their standard of living exorbitantly. They did not deplete their savings, using them for potential investments. They remained in their $60,000 home while accumulating $100,000 in CDs, mutual funds, annuities, and IRAs. They drove a buick and pick-up truck instead of two Mercedes. Today, George and Diane live in a $155,000 home, drive a truck and a Lincoln, and have over a $1,000,000 net worth. They are the epitome of financial wellness. By doing this, they have not set up a lifestyle that their money cannot outlive. They should be applauded for their financial results and planning that so few accomplish.

The average person should not try to build Rome in a day, but should take a simple and methodical approach to financial wellness. Remember to trust what you really want for yourself. Your banker, insurance agent, or stockbroker are all trying to make a living for their families. They do not always know what is right for you, if you do not know what is right for you. Educate yourself. Study this book. Buy some of the other education materials we recommend in the appendix. But most of all, decide what you truly need to experience the deep-down feelings of financial wellness. Be careful of someone selling you a great deal, whether it is the banker, insurance agent, or stockbroker.

The Country Mouse and the City Mouse

All of us are familiar with Aesop's fables. One particular story is appropriate in this chapter.

A quiet, country mouse once entertained an old playmate who had gone to the city to live. Though his wealth was very little, the country mouse saved up so that dinner for his city mouse friend would be a good one. He had put away some very nice peas and cheese and a tasty, ripe apple for dessert.

When he and his friend sat down to dinner, the country mouse didn't eat any food, but politely chewed away at a piece of straw, so that his city friend would be sure to have enough.

When they had finished, the city mouse said, in a very superior way, "How can you bear to live in such a dismal place? Nothing but woods, meadows, mountains, and streams. Don't you get bored with no society and no lively conversation? It must be awfully dull. Why don't you come to the city with me tonight? I'll show you how you can have a great time all of the time."

The little country mouse had always been perfectly content where he was, but he was willing to try something new.

So they set out that evening for the city. About midnight they walked into the beautiful mansion where the city mouse lived. There had been a great party the day before and bits of food were waiting for the picking.

They sat on beautiful Persian rugs and nibbled this and that until the country mouse was pleasantly full. He began to think that perhaps his life was pretty dull down there in the country.

Just then there was a bang and a crash that made them jump. The master of the house had come home. With him came two enormous dogs who barked and ran around, nearly scaring the life out of both the mice, who scurried for safety.

"Thank you ever so much," said the country mouse to his city friend. "That was fine while it lasted, but I think I'll just keep right on moving until I reach my quiet, dull little home back in the country. A few dry peas will do me very well as long as I can enjoy them quietly and not have my appetite scared out of me. You are welcome to your exciting city life, but I'll take the country."

———•••———

It's a wise person who has enough and is happy with it.

———•••———

Financial Dysfunction Leads to Dysfunctional Lifestyles

Financial issues, through either mismanagement or lack of employment, are some of the leading stresses in this country. Lack of financial stability leads to marital problems, drug abuse, eating disorders, alcohol addictions, and family or child abuse. Many people feel themselves searching for that quick financial fix through lotteries, gambling, or some other means of escaping financial devastation.

Depression and a feeling of loneliness or emptiness are common symptoms of people who are in financial quicksand. When their feelings start to take control of their lives, panic can cause a sane person to seek options that are no more than survival tactics—tactics such as white-collar crime, robbing a convenience store, lying and scheming a best friend. Obviously, this type of panic is a revolving door with no exit.

Dr. Charlesworth, in his book about "life management," has defined the effects our consumer, deficit-spending society has had on the American lifestyle. Our lives are terribly out of balance and in need of both emotional and spiritual redirection.

Definition of Dysfunctional Lifestyles

Dysfunctional lifestyle—

- a chronic and incessant pattern of living that is overinvolved in the pursuit of activities that the individual no longer finds purposeful, meaningful, emotionally rejuvenating, recreational, interpersonally satisfying, and healthful
- manifested by one or more of the following: overeating, overdrinking (or drugging)
  —overspending
  —physically endangering activities
  —physical neglect
  —narcissistic pursuit of physical perfection
  —emotional lability or isolation
  —reckless pursuit of hedonistic pleasure
  —lack of recreational pleasure
  —excess of competitive pursuits
  —poor prioritizing of meaningful activities
  —overcommitment of time
  —overly complicated structure of daily living, feelings of burnout, marital distress, job dissatisfaction, and/or feelings of being psychologically lost in life, all in a person of normal intelligence and emotional disposition.

Edward A. Charlesworth, Ph.D.

• • •

Financial Self-Responsibility

Over 90 percent of Americans are failing financially. We must stop and ask ourselves what to do about this problem. As we discussed earlier in this book, we must first stop and evaluate the situation. Ask yourselves these questions:

1. Is it my job that is holding me back?
2. Is it my spouse's fault I am failing?
3. Is it my personal mismanagement that is the problem?
4. Is it my lack of education that is holding me back?
5. Is it my boss that is holding me back?

It may be true that personal mismanagement is part of the problem; we may be our own greatest enemy when it comes to financial independence or responsibility. In our country, there is an old cliché—you can be anything you want to be and accomplish any goal that you set out to attain.

If it is truly the boss or job, then change jobs. But you must keep in mind that until you face yourself and decide what boundaries you will put on spending, you will not be in control of your financial destiny.

To achieve financial wellness, you must always pay yourself before anyone else is paid. This does not mean buy something you want personally, this means take a percentage of your monthly income and save it before the budget obligations are paid. You may say to that, "I cannot afford to pay myself." We say you *cannot afford not to* pay yourself first.

Many people in this country feel that security of financial issues and independence are created by their jobs. Actually, the security comes from within ourselves, and the job we have is merely a vehicle for reaching our goals.

One of the authors left school at the age of twenty-one to go into the insurance business, working on pure commission. Friends told him that he needed to work for the telephone company or be a fireman in order to have financial security in his future. It is interesting how they felt that security depended on the job. It is respectable to work for the telephone company or fire department, but there would be no reason to do it for security if someone really did not want to spend their life in that profession.

The other author was told he should not become a psychologist because it took too much education and there were no jobs available. He was told he would not make a lot of money if he decided to become a psychologist. He decided it was better to wake up every day and enjoy what he was doing, rather than live his life doing something he didn't like.

Both authors are working hard at their professions, raising families, and doing with their lives what they chose to give them a sense of purpose. Do not be guided by making money. Make money to live. Do not live to make money!

You should always remember that financial security is in your hands, not in the hands of someone else. Certainly you must understand that to achieve total financial wellness, you must not count on someone else to make it all better, for that is not going to happen. You have to take total control and responsibility for actions and face the *real* issues causing turmoil from within.

Financial Distress Can Lead to Emotional Wellness

It is almost impossible to say no to recreational consumerism if you do not have a burning, deep-down-inside yes about something truly important to your life. Have you ever noticed how when you have decided to do something worthwhile, it is easy to avoid shopping until you drop, reading or watching the advertisements, or participating in the gossip at the coffee machine? When we are committed to our goals, we can really "go for it." When our heart is burning with desire, we can "go for the gold."

This is a story about a person who had the desire to keep his family business going after the crash came with a bang. The Depression. The recession. Black Monday. Whatever way you add it up, it was devastating for this businessman, who recalled every day the feelings of panic when his family's contracting company nearly went bankrupt. Recession eliminated new building projects. He went from over fifty employees to only seven.

Lack of income was combined with pressure from banks to repay loans. He desperately looked for more business, became creative with his few dollars, and followed up diligently on all leads. He renegotiated with the banks. More jobs eventually came in and revenues began to increase.

Eight years later his income was seven times what it was before the recession. He stated defiantly, "Fear kicked up my survival instincts. I'm now still financially leaner than I was, I waste less, and I think more in terms of the long-term rather than the short-term. I feel better, like myself better, and have a stronger family life. It's really the people things that count."

This person let fear stir up his strong desire to succeed. He learned to say no to unnecessary expenses and time wasters. He learned that his true measure of worth did not come from fancy cars and watches, but from relationships, values, and ethics.

Poorly considered commitments may force you to spend money and time on things that don't matter. Learn what does matter and say no to the things that will not help you accomplish your goals and priorities in life.

- • • -

Men measure by the false standards that everyone
seeks power, success, riches for himself and admires

others who attain them while undervaluing the truly precious things in life.

Sigmund Freud

———— • • • ————

We are prone to judge success by the index of our salaries or the size of our automobiles rather than by the quality of our service and relationship to humanity.

Martin Luther King, Jr.

———— • • • ————

Don't Evaluate Your Success by Money

Who are the truly successful people? Perhaps they are the people who have found peace of mind and reached their greatest individual potential. These people seem to have lived lives where their actions and behaviors were in balance with their beliefs and values. And many such people may die with few material possessions. Mahatma Gandhi died possessing a pair of sandals, a staff, a spinning wheel, and glasses to read his prayer book. Yet we may all see him as a very successful person.

In a speech by trial attorney Dick King, we were reminded of what we lose in our materialistic society. He told a story about a trip he took to India for a Health, Hunger and Humanity project with Rotary International. He described visiting a very small, very poor village where the homes were cow-dung huts.

It was the custom to give a gift to your house guest. Knowing this custom prompted one of the members of the project to secretly give a gift to the guide, in turn to be given to the chief. Then the chief would have a gift to give away, and no one would have to know where it came from. However, the chief refused.

When the guests arrived at the chief's hut, they saw the chief, his wife holding a newborn baby, and their many children. The chief spoke through the interpreter, "A guest in your home is a God." He then looked around the barren hut, picked up a banged-up milk pail that was used to feed the children and gave it to the guests. Dick King reflected that the real gift that day was the handshake of a man of integrity and ethics.

— • • —

And there are those who have little and give it all. These are the believers in life and the bounty of life, and their coffer is never empty.

Kahlil Gibran
The Prophet

— • • —

Do not equate money with success. There are many successful money makers who are miserable failures as human beings.

Lloyd Shearer,
motivational speaker

— • • —

All a man has is his values . . . when he sells them out, he's got nothing left.

— • • —

Your Self-Esteem Is Based on Who You Are, Not What You Have

Sometimes finding our values amidst our confusion and conflicts is the catalyst to turn our lives around. We were reminded of this by a story about Darrel Teel, a drifter with only nine cents to his name. Darrel didn't have a home or job, and what money he did get was used to buy alcohol.

Then he found a handbag bulging with $29,200 cash in a field while he looked for cigarette butts. The money was the lost life savings of an elderly lady who just did not trust banks. Darrel's excitement and feeling of greed changed into soul-searching and then transformed into ethics. He turned the money in to the sheriff's department after thinking, "I don't steal. I'd like to earn this kind of money, but I don't steal."

This one act of honesty turned Darrel's life around. He received a citizen's award, the community raised $3,000 to help him start his life anew, and he had several job offers to select from. He quit drinking. Even his personality changed. With this one act of honesty, Darrel regained his self-respect, pride, and dignity.

— • • • —

You are what you are when nobody's looking.
Ann Landers

— • • • —

Pursue with Vigor What You Truly Value

Not all of us are going to define our purpose and value in the same way. Yet there is something to be gained by the attitude and outlook that sets our sights high and motivates us to live our life according to those goals and values. Mahatma Gandhi once said, "I have not the shadow of a doubt that any man or woman can achieve what I have if he or she would make the same effort." This reminds us of a ten-year-old girl who received a great humanitarian award for starting a petition to eliminate video games that promote hate and glorify figures such as Adolph Hitler. In her interview with ex-President Jimmy Carter she was poised, eloquent, and obviously committed to what she was doing. There is little we cannot accomplish when we are committed, instead of competitive.

Within each of us is the potential to live great, fulfilling lives. We have the power to shape the course of our destiny. Every day we are given twenty-four hours to spend, and those can be spent vigorously pursuing our true goals and values, or they can be spent unwisely. Once spent they are gone forever. When you examine truly great people, you find that they follow the dictates of their conscience, are in harmony with their values, and often dedicate a part of their life to serving their fellow man.

———•••———

How earnestly I must exert myself in order to give in return as much as I have received.

Albert Einstein

———•••———

Spend Your Time Wisely

When we work with clients, we try to emphasize that today they have twenty-four hours and that how they spend those 24 hours is a choice, conscious or unconscious. Though we may hope to live to be one hundred years old or older, we could be wrong and die today. So we should try to spend the time we have been given doing those things that fit our values. Live your life as if today were the last day of your life, and as if you are going to live to be one hundred years old!

———•••———

The measure of a man's life is the well spending of it,
and not the length.

Plutarch

————• • •————

Suburban Man and Meaning

The psychiatrist Rollo May, in his book *Man's Search for Himself* (Delacorte, 1973), describes the suburban man as one who "gets up at the same hour every weekday morning, takes the same train to work in the city, performs the same task at the office, lunches at the same place, leaves the same tip for the waitress each day, comes home on the same train each night, has 2.3 children, goes to church every Christmas and Easter, and moves through a routine mechanized existence year after year until he finally retires at sixty-five and very soon thereafter dies of heart failure."

What happens to us as we search for the American Dream? There is a type of pendulum that sometimes swings from "dropping out," through drugs or alternative lifestyles, to success, status, and wealth. Sometimes it swings back and forth.

Maybe workaholism makes our lives meaningless. Maybe not working hard creates an emptiness inside. Maybe, maybe not. What we do know is that living our life by our spiritual values and commitments will help us transcend financial dysfunction and soar into financial wellness.

————• • •————

Most men lead lives of quiet desperation.

Henry Thoreau

————• • •————

Leave Something Lasting for Your Children

Financial wellness also means a commitment to our children. The go-go-go of our deficit spending society and politicians has left a tremendous debt for our children. Become proactive in changing our society. Write your congressman or congresswoman. Speak out. Live your life in a financially responsible way.

One of our values is to leave our children the view of the world as a place of infinite opportunity and chances to do good. We, the authors, try to instill in our daughters how they may one day help make this world a better place. In every little thing they do they can express a desire to enhance the peace and betterment of mankind.

The founder of American psychology, William James, said, "The great use of life is to spend it for something that will outlast it." Money will not outlast our life if we do not learn to use it to serve mankind. We outlast life through our children, our ideas, and our deeds. The part of our value system that helps us survive the suffering and tragedies that befall us all is the belief that things may happen for a reason, and that it is my task to find that reason and make it meaningful. We do not always live in a just world. Rabbi Kushner clarified this beautifully in his book *Why Do Bad Things Happen to Good People?* We do not have that answer, but we believe that it all balances out in the end. The seeds we sow may be destroyed by drought, flood, or insects. But we keep planting if we believe that some of the seeds will grow.

• • •

To have a great purpose to work for, a purpose larger than ourselves, is one of the secrets of making life significant.

Will Durant

— • • • —

Possessions Won't Make This A Better World

There is a movie called *Saving Grace* in which Tom Conti plays the role of Pope Leo XIV who finds himself depressed, disconnected from the people, and questioning his real purpose. He leaves the Vatican and journeys, penniless and in street clothes, out into the countryside. There he reconnects with his purpose as he learns to serve people who are dejected, demoralized, and unmotivated.

In a place that has lost hope, he finds delinquents and derelicts. He desperately seeks to understand the people he leads. The seemingly simple task of helping them build an aqueduct to irrigate their fields and become self-sufficient rejuvenates his life and the lives of the people in the village.

In a warm, compassionate, humorous way the point is made that all the wealth of the Roman Catholic Church cannot make the pope happy if he is empty and disillusioned by his detachment from the true human condition. So it often seems to be with modern man. We are richer than ever before in terms of material possessions, but somehow we have lost our values and vision for the future. We have lost that which makes us feel whole and happy.

Unfortunately, by leaving it up to the popes and the governments of this world, we are losing the battle. We have delegated feeding the poor to under-funded, under-staffed programs. We want the police to make the neighborhoods safe. We have the nuclear bomb to make the world safe. But still we feel in danger, and well we should. If it's to be, it's up to me. Yes, that means you and me!

Leave The Bottle Full For Others

Years ago the Kingston Trio sang a song about a man who found a water pump out in the desert. If we remember correctly attached to the pump was a sign that said there was a jar of water hidden behind a rock for the purpose of priming the pump. The note went on to say that you might be tempted to drink the jar of water, but you had to use it to prime the pump in order to get more drinking water from the ground. The note ended by asking you to kindly leave the jar full of water for others who would pass by. The chorus of the song said, "You've got to prime that pump. You've got to have faith and believe." So it is with our financial life. Each of us has a responsibility to our financial life.

———— • • • ————

Leave the bottle full for others.

———— • • • ————

And He said to them, 'When I sent you without money bag, knapsack, and sandals, did you lack anything?" So they said, 'Nothing."

Luke 22:35

———— • • • ————

APPENDIX A

Personal **Financial** **Wellness** *Assessment*

About Mind Over Money, Inc.

The authors have formed a corporation to help people find products and services that will help them reach their financial goals. These products and services may include inexpensive computer software to budget your expenses and stay on top of your finances, or the latest in products to help you prepay your mortgage and refinance your home at a lower interest rate. Call us at 1–800–826–2723 to find out what is available.

Complete Financial Analysis

If you go to a financial advisor you could spend up to $1,500 for a complete financial analysis. By completing the following form and sending it to Mind Over Money, Inc., we will analyze your budget, financial statement, financial goals for retirement, needs for education of children, wants and desires (e.g., vacation homes, etc.), disability or life insurance needs, income needs if a family member dies prematurely, and help you establish a lifestyle to minimize your financial distress and put your "mind over money." Send $49.95 and your completed form to:

Mind Over Money, Inc.
P. O. Box 3594
Conroe, TX 77305

or call 1–800–826–2723 for more information.

PERSONAL *FINANCIAL WELLNESS* ASSESSMENT

Cut this out and mail to receive your personal financial wellness analysis in 4–6 weeks. A $1,500.00 value for $49.95.

I. Personal Data

	Head of Household	Spouse
Name		
Age		
Date of Birth		
Height/Weight		
Smoker/Non-smoker		
Health (good/poor)		
Social Security #		
Benefits (min./max.)		
Address		
Home Phone		
Occupation		
Employer & address		
Work Phone		
Name to appear on Financial Assessment		

	Name	Relationship	Date of Birth
Dependents			
1.			
2.			
3.			
4.			
5.			
6.			

Do you have a will?   ____ Yes   ____ No

Executor   _____

Guardian   _____

Trustees   _____

Do you own personal life insurance? ____ Yes   ____ No

Company   _____

Amount(s)   _____

Beneficiary   _____

Date Purchased   _____

YOUR EXPECTATIONS . . .

of the "long-term" inflation rate (3.5%–7.0%)?   _____

of your desired gain (after tax) or your investment
earnings?

   (circle one) 7%   8%   9%   10% and over

of the financial risks you're willing to take?

   (circle one)   1   2   3   4   5   6   7   8   9   10

          Low   High

Professional Advisors

Insurance planner: Name   _____

                 Agency   _____

                 Address _____

                              _____

                 Phone # _____

Accountant/CPA: Name   _____

                 Firm   _____

                 Address _____

                              _____

                 Phone # _____

Attorney: Name   _____

                 Firm   _____

                 Address   _____

                           _____

                 Phone #   _____

Banker: Name   _____

                 Bank   _____

                 Address   _____

                           _____

                 Phone #   _____

Trust Officer: Name   _____

                 Bank   _____

                 Address   _____

                           _____

                 Phone #   _____

II. FINANCIAL STATEMENT

	Current Value	Current Liabilities
Cash and Checking Accounts	$_____	$_____
T-Bills, Government Bonds and Money Market Funds	$_____	$_____
Savings Accounts & CDs	$_____	$_____
Municipal Bonds & Funds	$_____	$_____
Income Mutual Funds	$_____	$_____
Notes and Mortages Receivable	$_____	$_____
Life Insurance Cash Value	$_____	$_____
Tax Deferred Annuities	$_____	$_____
IRA, KEOGH, TSA, 401K	$_____	$_____
Corporate Qualified Plans (vested)	$_____	$_____
Residence	$_____	$_____
Common or Preferred Stock	$_____	$_____
Balanced Mutual Funds	$_____	$_____
Growth Mutual Funds	$_____	$_____
Variable Annuities	$_____	$_____
Income Property (Rental)	$_____	$_____
Undeveloped Land	$_____	$_____
Real Estate Partnerships	$_____	$_____
Energy Exploration Partnerships	$_____	$_____
Energy Income Partnerships	$_____	$_____
Equipment Lease, R&D and Tax Shelters	$_____	$_____
Business Interest (own a business)	$_____	$_____
Agriculture and Ranching	$_____	$_____
Art, Antiques, Stamps and Gems	$_____	$_____
Gold, Silver and Coins	$_____	$_____
Commodities	$_____	$_____
Miscellaneous Assets	$_____	$_____
Personal Property (clothing, furniture jewelry, etc.)	$_____	$_____

Automobiles (total value of all
vehicles) . . . . $_____ $_____
Recreational Property (boat, motorcycle,
camping, motorhome) . . . . $_____ $_____
Other Loans and Liabilities (including
credit cards) . . . . $_____ $_____

List credit cards and other loans   Amount Owed

1. _____   _____

2. _____   _____

3. _____   _____

4. _____   _____

5. _____   _____

                                                   Balance

Do you want the above current liabilities paid off at death?
____ Yes   ____ No

III. BUDGET

DOES YOUR BUDGET
MAKE GOOD "CENTS"?

1. Fill out income categories.
2. Fill out your estimated taxes.
3. Fill out your budget analyisis.
4. Subtract taxes (B) and budget total (C)
   from your total income (A).

SECTION A: INCOME

TAXABLE INCOME	RECEIVED MONTHLY	RECEIVED ANNUALLY
Salary (Head of Household)		
Salary (Spouse)		
Interest Income		
Stock Dividends		
Pensions and Alimony		
Bonus Income		
NON-TAXABLE INCOME		
Social Security		
Child Support, Municipal Bonds, etc.		
TOTAL RECEIPTS		

SECTION B: INCOME TAXES

	PAID MONTHLY	PAID ANNUALLY
Federal Income Tax (Head of Household)		
Federal Income Tax (Spouse)		
State Income Tax (Head of Household)		
State Income Tax (Spouse)		
F.I.C.A or Self-Employment Tax (Head of Household)		

F.I.C.A. or Self-
Employment Tax
(Spouse)   _____ _____
          TOTAL TAXES   _____ _____

SECTION C: PERSONAL EXPENSES

HOUSING:	ACTUAL AMOUNT	BUDGETED AMOUNT
Mortgage/Rent	_____	_____
Property Taxes	_____	_____
Homeowners Insurance	_____	_____
Homeowners Dues	_____	_____
Maintenance Dues	_____	_____
Utilities (includes: Cable Telephone, Gas, Water Electricity)	_____	_____
TOTAL	_____	_____
TRANSPORTATION:		
Car Payment(s)		
1.		
2.	_____	_____
3.	_____	_____
Car Insurance (total all vehicles)	_____	_____
Gasoline	_____	_____
Maintenance	_____	_____
License/Fees	_____	_____
TOTAL	_____	_____
HOUSEHOLD EXPENSES:		
Grocery	_____	_____
Clothing	_____	_____
Home Furnishings	_____	_____
Personal Care	_____	_____
Cash	_____	_____
Medical/Dental/Drugs	_____	_____
Medical Insurance	_____	_____
Life Insurance	_____	_____
Disability Insurance	_____	_____
Education Self-Improvement		
Child Care	_____	_____
TOTAL	_____	_____

ENTERTAINMENT:	ACTUAL AMOUNT	BUDGETED AMOUNT
Credit Cards	_____	_____
Dining Out/Movie/	_____	_____
Concert/Sporting	_____	_____
Event etc.	_____	_____
Recreational/Hobby	_____	_____
Equipment	_____	_____
Club Memberships/Dues	_____	_____
TOTAL	_____	_____
VACATION:		
Hotel	_____	_____
Travel	_____	_____
Dining	_____	_____
Amusement	_____	_____
TOTAL	_____	_____
HOLIDAYS:		
Christmas	_____	_____
Easter	_____	_____
Valentine's Day	_____	_____
Birthdays	_____	_____
TOTAL	_____	_____
CONTRIBUTIONS:		
Tithe	_____	_____
Charity	_____	_____
TOTAL	_____	_____
MISCELLANEOUS:		
_____	_____	_____
_____	_____	_____
_____	_____	_____
_____	_____	_____
TOTAL	_____	_____

GRAND TOTAL _____

What percentage is remaining _____%

✂ Subtract totals of B and C from A and divide your answer by A to get % of excess.

IV. INCOME TAX EVALUATION

Filing Status: Single
(circle one) Joint
            Head of Household
            Married, filing

	Head of Household	Spouse
Number of Exemptions	_____	_____
Number of Dependents		
Do you participate in a qualified retirement plan? Yes/No	_____	_____
State Income Tax Bracket	_____	_____
Federal Income Tax Bracket	_____	_____
Schedule C Total	_____	_____
Total Itemized Deductions	_____	_____
Annual Mortgate Interest and Taxes	_____	_____
Capital gains (+) or losses (-)	_____	_____
Federal Tax Credit Total Alternative Minimum Tax	_____	_____
PLUS or MINUS Adjustments	_____	_____
PLUS AMOUNT Preference	_____	_____
AMOUNT Foreign Tax Credits	_____	_____
State Income Taxes: Approximate Amount	_____	_____

V. DISABILITY

Disability Desires	Head of Household	Spouse
How long are you able to wait before disability benefits begin?	_____	_____
How long would you like to receive disability benefits?	_____	_____
How much per month do you need (before taxes from disability income?	_____	_____
Present Disability Coverage		
Company	_____	_____
Group/Personal Coverage	_____	_____
Waiting Period	_____	_____
Benefit Period	_____	_____
Monthly Benefit	_____	_____
Annual Premium	_____	_____

VI. HEALTH INSURANCE

Current Health Insurance	Head of Household	Spouse
Coverage	_____	_____
Annual Premium	_____	_____
Annual Deductible	_____	_____
Group or Individual (circle one)		

VII. LIFE INSURANCE

Name of Insured	Amount (Death Benefit)	Company	Type of Policy	Current Cash Value
1.				
2.				
3.				
4.				
5.				

VIII. FINANCIAL WELLNESS GOALS

A. College Funding

1. How much money would you like to make available for your children's education?_____
2. How much per year do you want to allow (in today's dollars) for college expenses?_____
3. List students and present age:

    _____
    _____
    _____

    The inflation rate you chose earlier will be used to figure your anticipated inflated college costs.

B. What Are Your Retirement Planning Needs?

1. At what age would you like to retire?_____
2. How much per month would you like to receive for retirement income (in today's dollars)?_____
3. Are you currently enrolled in a corporate retirement plan?_____
4. Do you have an IRA?   Yes/No
    Where: _____

    Do you want us to use social security income as we calculate your retirement income.   Yes/No
    At what age do you plan to draw social security?
                                                    62 or 65
    What is your estimated monthly income from company pension (in today's dollars)?_____
    At what age does it begin?_____
    How much are you currently saving per month for retirement?_____

C. Future Inheritance

What is estimated value?_____
At what age do you expect to receive these benefits?
_____

D. Short Term Goals

	When Payoff Needed?	How Much Needed for Payoff?
1. Payoff of home early	_____	_____
2. Vacation home/new cars/etc.	_____	_____
3. Other	_____	_____

IX. NEEDS FOR SURVIVORS

A. What Are Your Cash Expense Needs in the Event of a Death?

	Amount
Burial and final medical expenses	_____
Attorney fees and probate costs	_____
Emergency fund (90 days budget expenses	_____
Mortgage fund (to pay off mortgage on house)	_____
Debt retirement (pay off liabilities)	_____
College and continued education	_____
Miscellaneous	_____

B. What Are Your Cash Income Needs in the Event of a Death?

Income necessary for family to maintain present lifestyle.

	Survivor with dependents living at home	Survivor with dependents not at home
How much income can you provide?		
Head of Household	_____	
Spouse	_____	_____
How much do you need in income?		
Head of Household	_____	
Spouse	_____	_____

APPENDIX B

Financial Physical Checklist

FINANCIAL PHYSICAL CHECKLIST

Instructions: Please mark the appropriate boxes applicable to your situation. Return this with your Financial Wellness Assessment form for maximum benefit analysis.

- ☐ Have life insurance program
- ☐ Have group medical insurance
- ☐ Have homeowners insurance
- ☐ Have outstanding loans on insurance
- ☐ Have checked beneficiary information in past five years
- ☐ Have had a complete financial analysis
- ☐ Have a written budget
- ☐ Have a will
- ☐ Have additional insurance protection for family members
- ☐ Have mutual funds
- ☐ Have tax-deferred annuities
- ☐ Have an IRA (Individual Retirement Plan)
- ☐ Have a 401K retirement plan
- ☐ Have a 403B plan for teachers/ministers
- ☐ Have a SEP plan (Simplified Employment)
- ☐ Have disability insurance
- ☐ Have a college fund for children
- ☐ Have been accelerating mortgage
- ☐ Have considered pre-conversion of group term ins.
- ☐ Have checked my social security account
- ☐ Have performed credit card debt consolidation

✂ NAME: _____

ADDRESS: _____

Phone: _____ W

_____ H

APPENDIX C

Life Insurance Samples

Term Insurance Sample

The following is an example of term insurance bought over forty years. As discussed earlier, term insurance is more advantageous for short-term needs as opposed to long-term ones. Column "A" shows the dramatic increase in cost to the consumer, which escalates after age 55. Many people buy term insurance with intentions of investing the difference. However, most people never follow through with their intended investments. As they get older, the premium prices escalate and they drop their insurance policies before they die. This, in turn, makes term insurance very profitable for the companies that provide it. Notice the total at the bottom of column "A." This is the combination of all premiums paid from age 35 to age 75.

		A	B	C	D
Year	Age	Annual Premium with Reentry	Annual Premium without Reentry	Guaranteed Maximum Premium	Death Benefit
1	36	290	290	290	200,000
2	37	290	290	290	200,000
3	38	290	290	290	200,000
4	39	290	290	290	200,000
5	40	290	290	290	200,000
6	41	290	290	290	200,000
7	42	290	290	290	200,000
8	43	290	290	290	200,000
9	44	290	290	290	200,000
10	45	290	290	290	200,000
		2,900	2,900		

Year	Age	A Annual Premium with Reentry	B Annual Premium without Reentry	C Guaranteed Maximum Premium	D Death Benefit
11	46	564	1,012	1,430	200,000
12	47	564	1,046	1,542	200,000
13	48	564	1,082	1,662	200,000
14	49	564	1,118	1,794	200,000
15	50	564	1,154	1,938	200,000
16	51	564	1,194	2,102	200,000
17	52	564	1,298	2,290	200,000
18	53	564	1,414	2,506	200,000
19	54	564	1,550	2,754	200,000
20	55	564	1,704	3,030	200,000
		8,540	15,472		
21	56	1,872	1,872	3,338	200,000
22	57	2,060	2,060	3,674	200,000
23	58	2,260	2,260	4,030	200,000
24	59	2,478	2,478	4,426	200,000
25	60	2,722	2,722	4,870	200,000
26	61	2,994	2,994	5,366	200,000
27	62	3,298	3,298	5,918	200,000
28	63	3,644	3,644	6,554	200,000
29	64	4,036	4,036	7,274	200,000
30	65	4,480	4,480	8,074	200,000
		38,384	45,316		
31	66	4,972	4,972	8,950	200,000
32	67	5,504	5,504	9,898	200,000
33	68	6,076	6,076	10,914	200,000
34	69	6,692	6,692	12,018	200,000
35	70	7,362	7,362	13,242	200,000
36	71	8,120	8,120	14 626	200,000
37	72	9,116	9,116	16,206	200,000
38	73	9,966	9,966	18,034	200,000
39	74	11,102	11,102	20,094	200,000
40	75	12,380	12,380	22,362	200,000
		119,674	126,606		

Whole Life Sample

The following sample is a whole life insurance proposal. This policy does not have an escalating premium like that of a term insurance policy (notice the "Annualized Premium" column). You can accrue a Guaranteed Cash Value, which is basically an escrowing of your premiums. The Total Cash Value column shows the total of your Guaranteed Cash Value plus any Annual Dividend you may receive. The "Death Benefit" column increases with the worth of your policy. If you choose to leave the plan, you may receive your Total Cash Value at that time. Note: Whole life will typically be your highest premium policy per $1,000 of insurance coverage. This policy in today's market has become a *dinosaur*.

End of Year	Age	Annualized Premium	Annual Dividend	Gtd Cash Value	Total Cash Value	Death Benefit
1	36	1,460	0	0	0	100,000
2	37	1,460	57	0	57	100,057
3	38	1,460	101	800	964	100,164
4	39	1,460	185	1,800	2,165	100,365
5	40	1,460	292	3,000	3,691	100,691
6	41	1,460	406	4,100	5,261	101,161
7	42	1,460	506	5,300	7,075	101,775
8	43	1,460	598	6,600	9,139	102,539
9	44	1,460	690	7,900	11,365	103,465
10	45	1,460	781	9,200	13,769	104,569
		14,596				
11	46	1,460	871	10,600	16,465	105,865
12	47	1,460	959	12,000	19,368	107,368
13	48	1,460	1,040	13,400	22,493	109,093

End of Year	Age	Annualized Premium	Annual Dividend	Gtd Cash Value	Total Cash Value	Death Benefit
14	49	1,460	1,123	14,900	25,961	111,061
15	50	1,460	1,207	16,400	29,695	113,295
16	51	1,460	1,288	18,000	33,817	115,817
17	52	1,460	1,376	19,600	38,262	118,662
18	53	1,460	1,462	21,300	43,156	121,856
19	54	1,460	1,553	23,000	48,438	125,438
20	55	1,460	1,643	24,700	54,143	129,443
		29,191				
21	56	1,460	1,728	26,500	60,404	133,904
22	57	1,460	1,823	28,200	67,074	138,874
23	58	1,460	1,916	30,100	74,499	144,399
24	59	1,460	2,011	31,900	82,431	150,531
25	60	1,460	2,103	33,800	91,125	157,325
26	61	1,460	2,171	35,700	100,517	164,817
27	62	1,460	2,251	37,600	110,685	173,085
28	63	1,460	2,361	39,600	121,830	182,230
29	64	1,460	2,511	41,500	133,874	192,374
30	65	1,460	2,711	43,500	147,160	203,660
		43,787				
31	66	1,460	2,975	45,400	161,657	216,257
32	67	1,460	3,276	47,400	177,724	230,325
33	68	1,460	3,581	49,400	195,402	246,002
34	69	1,460	3,897	51,300	214,752	263,452
35	70	1,460	4,222	53,300	236,146	282,846
36	71	1,460	4,444	55,200	259,462	304,262
37	72	1,460	4,669	57,200	285,092	327,892
38	73	1,460	4,892	59,100	313,037	353,937
39	74	1,460	5,116	60,900	343,524	382,624
40	75	1,460	5,336	62,700	376,894	414,194
		58,382				
41	76	1,460	5,537	64,500	413,394	448,894
42	77	1,460	5,705	66,200	453,184	486,984
43	78	1,460	5,859	67,800	496,563	528,763
44	79	1,460	6,025	69,500	544,086	574,586
45	80	1,460	6,176	71,000	595,814	624,814

End of Year	Age	Annualized Premium	Annual Dividend	Gtd Cash Value	Total Cash Value	Death Benefit
46	81	1,460	6,310	72,600	652,438	679,838
47	82	1,460	6,399	74,100	714,158	740,058
48	83	1,460	6,488	75,600	781,557	805,957
49	84	1,460	6,546	77,000	855,031	878,031
50	85	1,460	6,603	78,300	935,152	956,852
		72,978				

Variable Life Sample

The following is a sample of variable life insurance bought for a $100,000 death benefit, tracking the progress of the policy over a twenty year period. Variable life policies combine investment products and life insurance. In a variable life policy, the consumer has a choice as to where he or she may invest. Many 401K plans are variations of a variable life policy.

The yearly premium for this example is $866.00. This sample gives three different annual return percentage examples. The three columns marked "B" show a 0.00 percent return on your investment (a worst case scenario). The columns marked "C" show a conservative return on your investment of 8.00 percent. The columns marked "D" show a possible mutual fund return of 12.00 percent. The example in the columns marked "B", if extended to age 71, shows that the 0.00 percent return runs out of money and the premiums must increase. This leads to a WARNING: Always review your Annual Earnings Statement in order to avoid poor returns. Change your investment choice if the earnings are unacceptable.

	A		B Assumed Gross Annual Return of 0.00%			C Assumed Gross Annual Return of 8.00%			D Assumed Gross Annual Return of 12.00%		
Yr.	Age	Annual. Planned Premium	Surren- der Value	Accum. Value	Death Benefit	Surren- der Value	Accum. Value	Death Benefit	Surren- der Value	Accum. Value	Death Benefit
1	36	866.00	242	569	100,000	296	623	100,000	323	650	100,000
2	37	866.00	795	1,122	100,000	991	1,278	100,000	1.032	1,359	100,000
3	38	866.00	1,329	1,656	100,000	1,637	1,964	100,000	1,804	2,131	100,000
4	39	866.00	1,885	2,171	100,000	2,396	2,682	100,000	2,685	2,971	100,000
5	40	866.00	2,420	2,666	100,000	3,190	3,435	100,000	3,641	3,886	100,000
6	41	866.00	2,934	3,138	100,000	4,017	4,221	100,000	4,677	4,882	100,000
7	42	866.00	3,424	3,588	100,000	4,879	5,042	100,000	5,082	5,965	100,000
8	43	866.00	3,891	4,014	100,000	5,777	5,900	100,000	7,923	7,146	100,000
9	44	866.00	4,334	4,413	100,000	6,713	4,795	100,000	8,351	8,432	100,000
10	45	866.00	4,753	4,794	100,000	7,692	7,733	100,000	9,798	9,838	100,000
11	46	806,90	5,154	5,154	100,000	8,719	8,719	100,000	11,380	11,380	100,000
12	47	866.00	5,492	5,492	100,000	9,755	9,755	100,000	13,071	13,071	100,000
13	48	866.00	5,810	5,810	100,000	10,845	10,845	100,000	14,928	14,928	100,000
14	49	866.00	6,107	6,107	100,000	11,992	11,992	100,000	16,968	16,968	100,000
15	50	866.00	6,381	6,381	100,000	13,199	13,199	100,000	19,211	19,211	100,000
16	51	866.00	6,631	6,631	100,000	14,469	14,469	100,000	21,678	21,678	100,000
17	52	866.00	6,857	6,857	100,000	15,805	15,805	100,000	24,394	24,394	100,000
18	53	866.00	7,055	7,055	100,000	17,211	17,211	100,000	27,384	27,384	100,000
19	54	866.00	7,226	7,226	100,000	18,691	18,691	100,000	30,680	30,680	100,000
20	55	866.00	7,369	7,369	100,000	20,251	20,251	100,000	34,316	34,316	100,000
			INSUFFICIENT PREMIUMS PAST AGE 71			MATURES AT ANNIVERSARY AFTER AGE 95			MATURES AT ANNIVERSARY AFTER AGE 95		

Universal Life Policy

The following illustration is a Universal Life policy. As we discussed eralier, the Universal Life option allows you to have the flexibility of designing your own policy. You pay only the premium that you can afford, and the insurance company will tell you the amount of coverage that can be purchased at your given age. After the Annualized Premium is determined, two examples of investment returns are given. One estimate shows the "Guaranteed" rate of 4.00 percent (the insurance company will not let the policy go below this). The other estimate shows the "current" rate of 6.9 percent. This short sample chart reveals that this 35 year-old male with these low premiums will be required to pay more premium at age 51 on a 4.00 percent return on his policy. REMEMBER: Have your agent extend your affordable premium amount to age 70 at the lowest "Guaranteed" rate. This will initially protect you from possible poor planning. Don't assume interest earnings will always stay at the "current" level.

End of Year	Age	Annual. Premium	[——Guaranteed 4.000%——]			[——Current 6.900%——]		
			Sur. Value	Accum. Value	Death Benefit	Sur. Value	Accum. Value	Death Benefit
1	36	442	0	190	100,000	0	224	100,000
2	37	442	0	380	100,000	0	457	100,000
3	38	442	0	565	100,000	0	693	100,000
4	39	442	0	744	100,000	0	932	100,000
5	40	442	0	917	100,000	201	1,176	100,000
6	41	300	135	947	100,000	468	1,280	100,000
7	42	300	310	959	100,000	725	1,374	100,000
8	43	300	466	953	100,000	976	1,463	100,000
9	44	300	601	926	100,000	1,220	1,545	100,000
10	45	300	712	874	100,000	1,453	1,615	100,000
		3,710						
11	46	300	794	794	100,000	1,669	1,669	100,000
12	47	300	682	682	100,000	1,701	1,701	100,000
13	48	300	534	534	100,000	1,710	1,710	100,000
14	49	300	346	346	100,000	1,698	1,698	100,000
15	50	300	114	114	100,000	1,666	1,666	100,000
16	51	300	0	0	0	1,612	1,612	100,000
17	52	300	0	0	0	1,534	1,534	100,000
18	53	300	0	0	0	1,422	1,422	100,000
19	54	300	0	0	0	1,266	1,266	100,000
20	55	300	0	0	0	1,062	1,062	100,000
		6,710						
21	56	300	0	0	0	813	813	100,000
22	57	300	0	0	0	524	524	100,000
23	58	300	0	0	0	188	188	100,000
		7,610						

Adjustable Life Sample

The adjustable life policy has much of the flexibility typical of the Universal Life option. In comparison to Universal Life, Adjustable Life policies are not as easy to find. However, this policy is one of the authors' favorites. The premium in most cases should not increase. The "Total Cash Value" column is the Guaranteed Cash Value plus the dividends you will receive in any given year. The "Paid-Up Death Benefit" column (which could have been shown on the other samples) is the amount of benefits a person could receive if he or she quit the plan that year. If a person abandoned the plan at age 50, he or she would have a choice between $5,389 in cash or a deferred, already paid-up death benefit of $13,896 after death. RE-MEMBER: When purchasing an Adjustable Life Policy, make sure it pays dividends and has a Cost of Living Index. This Index will allow you to increase your coverage regardless of medical problems. Usually this feature is not found on most Whole, Universal, or Term Life policies.

Year	Age	Initial Annualized Premium	Plan Gtd. Cash Value	Total Cash Value	Death Benefit	Paid-Up Death Benefit
1	36	497	0	0	100,000	
2	37	497	106	124	100,000	492
3	38	497	205	263	100,000	1,004
4	39	497	295	438	100,000	1,616
5	40	497	375	669	100,000	2,388
6	41	497	441	953	100,000	3,289
7	42	497	491	1,291	100,000	4,310
8	43	497	523	1,681	100,000	5,431
9	44	497	536	2,128	100,000	6,652
10	45	497	526	2,603	100,000	7,876
		4,977				

Year	Age	Initial Annualized Premium	Plan Gtd. Cash Value	Total Cash Value	Death Benefit	Paid-Up Death Benefit
11	46	497	489	3,104	100,000	9,092
12	47	497	422	3,629	100,000	10,292
13	48	497	321	4,181	100,000	11,486
14	49	497	182	4,766	100,000	12,682
15	50	497	0	5,389	100,000	13,896
16	51	497	0	6,056	100,000	15,134
17	52	497	0	6,765	100,000	16,388
18	53	497	0	7,520	100,000	17,667
19	54	497	0	8,316	100,000	18,953
20	55	497 _9,955_	0	9,154	100,000	20,249
21	56	497	0	10,045	100,000	21,573
22	57	497	0	10,999	100,000	22,945
23	58	497	0	12,022	100,000	24,373
24	59	497	0	13,132	100,000	25,881
25	60	497	0	14,287	100,000	27,385
26	61	497	0	15,478	100,000	28,870
27	62	497	0	16,714	100,000	30,351
28	63	497	0	18,060	100,000	31,945
29	64	497	0	19,445	100,000	33,530
30	65	497 _14,932_	0	20,881	100,000	35,113
31	66	497	0	22,369	100,000	36,711
32	67	497	0	23,924	100,000	38,343
33	68	497	0	25,551	100,000	40,013
34	69	497	0	27,240	100,000	41,707
35	70	497	0	28,998	100,000	43,433
36	71	497	0	30,770	100,000	45,115
37	72	497	0	32,593	100,000	46,813
38	73	497	0	34,463	100,000	48,528
39	74	497	0	36,375	100,000	50,260
40	75	497 _19,910_	0	38,325	100,000	52,008
41	76	497	0	40,308	100,000	53,767
42	77	497	0	42,309	100,000	55,518
43	78	497	0	44,294	100,000	57,217

Year	Age	Initial Annualized Premium	Plan Gtd. Cash Value	Total Cash Value	Death Benefit	Paid-Up Death Benefit
44	79	497	0	46,252	100,000	58,849
45	80	497	0	48,163	100,000	60,395
46	81	497	0	49,977	100,000	61,800
47	82	497	0	51,614	100,000	62,977
48	83	497	0	53,056	100,000	63,925
49	84	497	0	54,277	100,000	64,626
50	85	497	0	55,321	100,000	65,146
		24,888				